Lord, Teach Us to Pray

A Study of Personal Prayer

Romans 8:26-27

We do not know what we ought to pray for but the Spirit himself intercedes for us with groans that words can not express. And he who searches our hearts knows the mind of the Spirit, because the Spirit intercedes for the saints in accordance with Gods will.

As a believer, you are not left to your own resources to cope with problems. Even when you don't know the right words to pray, The Holy Spirit prays with you and for you, and God answers. With God helping you to pray, you don't need to be afraid to come before him. Ask The Holy Spirit to intercede for you, in accordance with Gods will. God will always do what is best.

Cover design by Shawn Lancaster
Interior design by PerfecType, Nashville, TN
ISBN 978-0-88177-570-9
Library of Congress Control Number 2009921846

371 - Church
372 - TBN
373 - word
369 - Way Star
367 - WHJ
364 Imap

Contents

344 - SWAGGART

HEB - 4:16
2 Corinth. 5:18-21

Becoming Prayerful

As believers, we are all becoming people of prayer. Although we have not reached perfection, we should all know where we are headed. What is our goal as Christians? Simply put—to become daily more and more like Christ.

Our faith journey involves making steps toward becoming more like Christ. Each one of us walks with God in unique ways and each of us has our own faith story. Some of us take giant steps, at times we seem to be growing exponentially; at other times our walk consists of baby steps. Honestly, sometimes our progress is halted, or we may even appear to go backwards.

My prayer as you read this book is that you will choose to take another step toward maturity in your personal prayer life. Teaching and testimony combine to make an effective witness. Therefore, I will include parts of my own story with the scriptural teaching on personal prayer. I believe faith sharing builds faith. My desire is to be a living epistle, sharing both my victories with the Lord and the ways that I have struggled to know intimacy with God through prayer. The clarion call of the Holy Spirit in this day is for believers to walk in intimacy with God. That is the longing of my heart, and I trust it is your desire as well.

CHAPTER ONE

Stages of Prayer: "A Pilgrim's Progress"

We can be mature in one area of our Christian walk, and still be a beginner in other areas. That is not an indictment, but an acknowledgment of the different ways we grow. If we are still a beginner in our prayer life, God simply desires us to take the next step toward confidence in the power of prayer. God, through the power of the Holy Spirit, is at work to help us make progress. We are not striving in our own strength. God desires and provides for an intimate prayer life for all believers.

My pilgrim's progress is probably different from yours, but we all share three basic stages of prayer: (1) pre-Christian prayer, (2) transition prayer, and (3) confident prayer.

We all begin at stage one, *pre-Christian prayer*. Did you ever talk to God before you invited Jesus to become your personal

Savior? If you did, you experienced pre-Christian prayer. Some of us spent a lot more time in this period than others. It is possible some of us may never have made a personal commitment to Jesus and prayed the salvation prayer; therefore, we would still be in stage one.

Pre-Christian prayers are characterized by elementary prayers. You may have childhood remembrances of elementary prayers like "God bless Mommy, God bless Daddy; Now I lay me down to sleep; God is good, God is great, let us thank him for this food." Elementary prayers can be powerful. God hears them! God loves children's prayers because they are so honest and real. They have no hidden agenda.

Ritualistic and emergency prayers may also characterize this first stage of prayer. Ritualistic prayers are those prayers we memorize, like the Lord's Prayer. We repeat them often as a way of communicating with God. These ritualistic and liturgical prayers definitely have a place in our prayer lives. They can teach us the faith of generations before us and give us a framework for learning how to talk to God. They help us voice what's in our heart. But, they are not meant to be a substitute for personally talking with God. If you grew up in the church, you likely learned many ritualistic prayers. I trust they helped rather than hindered your prayer life.

Emergency prayers are those exclamations lifted to God at points of desperation in our life. Again, they can be very real and meaningful. Prayers like, "Help me, God," or "God, I need you" have the potential to touch God's heart and bring a speedy response. No doubt, they have a place in our prayer life.

For each of us, the pre-Christian prayer stage ends as we make a personal commitment to Jesus Christ as our Lord and Savior. For some of us, we return to God like the prodigal son in Luke 15:20. What hope this scripture gives us.

"So he set off and went to his father. But while he was still far off, his father saw him and was filled with compassion; he ran and put his arms around him and kissed him." (Luke 15:20)

The Father responds to us even before we see him, while we are still a long way off. When we return to God, our Father is filled with compassion and readily receives us.

Praying a salvation prayer dramatically changes our life! We begin a personal relationship with God, and often move from elementary prayers addressed to a vague and distant, perhaps ominous God, into a personal desire to communicate with our Savior. Prayer often takes on a new priority.

When the LORD *saw that he had turned aside to see, God called to him out of the bush, "Moses, Moses!" And he said, "Here I am."* (Exodus 3:4)

After salvation, we move into the second stage, *transition prayer*. Like Moses in Exodus 3:4, we often turn aside to take a closer look at prayer at this time. It is significant to notice that Moses took the first step, and then God called to him. Moses made a decision to turn and take a closer look, even though what he was seeing was strange and unfamiliar to him. Many of us may be where Moses was in Exodus 3.

This second stage in prayer may be accompanied by uncomfortable or unfamiliar feelings as we step out in new and unfamiliar ways of praying, of relating to God, and being obedient to him. We need to be honest about any uncomfortable feelings that may be associated with desiring to go deeper in prayer. During this stage, we are often tempted by comparison to others. We may also fall into the trap of judging our prayer life against more mature people of prayer. Unfortunately, this may lead to feelings of inadequacy. We can experience embarrassment at our beginner status and even a temptation to quit praying. That is not God's way. God loves us dearly during this transition period and wants us to come to him in prayer.

But if you will look to God and plead with the Almighty, if you are pure and upright, even now he will rouse himself on your behalf and restore you to your rightful place. Your beginnings will seem humble, so prosperous will your future be. (Job 8:5-7, NIV, emphasis added.)

God also promises us growth. The promise of Job 8:5-7 speaks to our desire to grow in prayer. Acknowledging how much we have to learn and humbly asking God to teach us to pray bring many rewards. Often this will lead us directly into the third stage of prayer: a breakthrough into *confident prayer*. We can again use Moses as an example of maturing in prayer. From his humble beginnings, Moses became a mighty example of prayer. From Exodus 7:6, 10, 20 we see that Moses learned obedience in his relationship with God: "Moses . . . *did just as the* LORD *had commanded*" (italics added).

As we are obedient to what God has told us in prayer, our relationship with God grows in intimacy. We become more confident in our ability to hear God and to know his will for our lives. What was the last thing God told you in prayer? Did you obey? The true test of maturity in our prayer life is obedience.

As I reflect on these stages of prayer, I am reminded of my own prayer journey, my *pilgrim's progress*. I spent seventeen years in the first stage of prayer. Because I did not grow up in a

Christian family, church and the ways of God were foreign to me. I have some early childhood remembrances of prayer when I had opportunities to visit churches, especially at Christmas and Easter. Mostly I saw formal, liturgical prayers modeled. I never remember hearing that God loved me and had a wonderful plan for my life. I do, however, have some early memories of emergency prayers. Especially at times of deep feelings of loneliness and rejection, I remember crying out, "Where are you, God?"

As a teenager, God brought some faithful witnesses to illustrate unconditional love to me. Twin girls, friends from school, showed me the love of God when I was very difficult to love. I know now that they prayed earnestly for me. I find it so ironic that God has given me a passion for prayer that I believe began as I was a recipient of heartfelt prayer and intercession.

At the age of seventeen, during an evangelistic meeting I heard the plan of salvation for the first time. And wonder of wonders, I gave my life to God that day; I asked Jesus to be my personal Savior. From that day forward, my life has never been the same. I brought a lot of baggage into my newfound relationship with Jesus. Feelings of rejection and low self-esteem hindered my walk with God and affected my prayer life. I definitely struggled with feelings of inadequacy and comparison of my prayer life with others. I remained in this second stage, transition prayer, for many years.

But God! Don't you just love the *but God* points in your life? *But God* provided for my growth. Miraculously, my husband, Harry, and I were moved to a truly alive church in Wisconsin. There I began to find healing from my past, growth in all areas of my spiritual life, and strong teaching about the person and work of the Holy Spirit.

It was during this time that I entered the third stage of prayer. I made a breakthrough into the confidence in prayer when I was baptized in the Holy Spirit. After I was baptized in the Holy Spirit, I began to understand how to hear God's voice. For the first time in my life, prayer really became a conversation. I am also so thankful for the heritage of obedience I learned under my beloved pastor during this time.

We often teased our pastor that he only had one sermon— "Total Commitment." He faithfully taught us that we could never really know Christ until we were willing to totally commit our lives to God. That is the truth. He preached often about obedience, which we lovingly called "The Big O." We must totally commit our lives to Christ to be born of the Spirit. Then, we must walk in obedience to God. Obedience is the only way to walk in the power of the Holy Spirit.

These three stages of prayer are not rigid steps in our journey to become people of prayer. They do, however, help us to reflect honestly about where we are in our personal prayer life. Even after we have made a breakthrough into confident prayer, for example, we can go back at times to feelings of inadequacy and comparison characteristic of the transition period. We may never eliminate emergency prayers that are characteristic of the first stage of prayer. Those prayers are honest and valid communication with God regardless of our maturity in prayer. We should not expect to leave liturgical prayers behind as we progress toward confidence in the power of prayer. A well-balanced prayer life will likely contain all of these elements.

Stay the course, pilgrim. Intimacy with God through prayer is our goal and the Holy Spirit is God's provision for our progress.

Questions for Personal Reflection

1. Think about the stages of prayer, and assess where you are in your own *pilgrim's progress*. What will help you take the next step of growth in your prayer life?

2. Think about your current prayer life. What is your greatest strength? What is a current weakness? What steps can you take to overcome this current weakness?

3. Like Moses in Exodus 3, we can turn aside to take a closer look at God. Think about a time in your own life that you turned aside to seek God in prayer. What were the circumstances? What were the results?

4. How has the Holy Spirit been at work in your prayer life?

Activities for Small Groups

1. Thank God for giving Jesus as our means for a personal relationship with God through prayer.

2. Pray for one another. Ask God to help you develop the intimacy in prayer that he desires.

CHAPTER TWO

Christian Prayer Is . . .

Every world religion contains an element of prayer. However, clearly not all prayer is Christian prayer. When we discuss prayer, we need to be sure we are operating from the same perspective. Without attempting to be deeply theological, we need to be clear about the distinctive nature of Christian prayer. How we think about prayer really does have an affect on our practice of prayer. Let's look at three distinct aspects of Christian prayer.

Christian prayer is direct communication with God. Talking with and listening to God are both important aspects of prayer. As you evaluate your prayer life, which area is strongest for you? Where do you need the most improvement? For many, listening in prayer is the weakest area. We'll spend time on this topic here and in Unit Three.

What is communication? A dictionary definition of communication gives us hope as we strive to grow in our ability to listen in prayer: "To communicate is to transmit information, thoughts, or feelings so that there is understanding between the communicating parties." This definition reminds us that without understanding, communication has not taken place. Communication with understanding is necessary in our relationships with other people and in our relationship with God.

The good news is that God wants to communicate with us. God goes to great lengths to help us know his will and discern his voice. We can be confident that God will communicate with us in such a way that we will understand.

Listening to God is not complicated. However, we need to understand that God speaks to us in a variety of ways. These ways include the Bible; visions, dreams, impressions, and thoughts; and other people.

Let us therefore approach the throne of grace with boldness, so that we may receive mercy and find grace to help in time of need. (Hebrews 4:16)

Let's not take for granted our need to talk to God. Many of us also need to grow in this aspect of prayer. Basic questions arise as we begin to understand communicating with God. What do I say? Are all topics acceptable? Can I be emotionally real—saying what I really think to the God of the universe? Hebrews 4:16 is helpful as we think about our ability to come to God in prayer. We need to learn, or perhaps rethink, how we come to God. Do you come before God with boldness, confident that you will receive his grace, mercy, and help when you pray? This is our place as redeemed children of the King.

For God so loved the world that he gave his only Son, so that everyone who believes in him may not perish but may have eternal life. (John 3:16)

Christian prayer demonstrates belief in the character and nature of our God. This truth is another important distinction of Christian prayer. The God we serve is Father, Son, and Holy Spirit. All three aspects of God's character have a deep affect on our prayers. God the Father desires a love relationship with all humanity, and sent his Son to bridge the gap between finite man and infinite Almighty God. The familiar words of John 3:16 make that clear, and the impact of this verse underscores the truth that prayer is a relationship! God the Father went to great lengths to provide for a love relationship with us. Our prayer life should be a reflection of this intimate relationship. We become familiar with our holy God as we spend time in prayer. How important is a love relationship with God in your prayer life? Examine your prayers with the insight that God sent Jesus to provide a means for a personal relationship with you. How much time in your prayer life is devoted to nurturing or sustaining this love relationship?

He is the reflection of God's glory and the exact imprint of God's very being, and he sustains all things by his powerful word. When he had made purification for sins, he sat down at the right hand of the Majesty on high. (Hebrews 1:3)

Another distinction of Christian prayer is our relationship with Jesus. Christian prayer must be based on God the Son. Hebrews 1:3 shows us that Jesus upholds and sustains all life by his powerful word. This verse further affirms the mystery of the incarnation: Jesus was both fully God and fully man—"the exact imprint of God's very being." Where is Jesus now? Jesus, in his resurrection body, is seated beside the Father in heaven. What is Jesus' role in heaven? Jesus is praying for us! How does this truth affect your personal communication with God? Examine your current prayer life from the perspective that Jesus' *job description* for all eternity is to be interceding for you (Hebrews 7:25).

The third person of the Trinity, the Holy Spirit, also deeply affects our prayer life. Understanding the person and work of the Holy Spirit is vital to our practice of prayer. The Holy Spirit was released by the Father to hover over the waters and to be present at creation. Genesis 1:2 reminds us that the truth of the Holy Spirit was not reserved for the New Testament. The Holy Spirit did not suddenly appear on the scene at Pentecost. Rather, God's Holy Spirit was at work from the very beginning of creation. In the Old Testament, however, the Holy Spirit was not available for all. Instead, God's Spirit came upon certain individuals for a specific task. Leaders like Moses and prophets like Isaiah experienced the anointing of the Holy Spirit. But God's Spirit had not yet been poured out for all.

By God's grace, that changed with Pentecost. The Holy Spirit can now empower and indwell every believer. We do not have to rely on our own strength in any area of our spiritual life. The Holy Spirit is available to lead us into all truth. Consider John 16:13.

"When the Spirit of truth comes, he will guide you into all the truth; for he will not speak on his own, but will speak whatever he hears, and he will declare to you the things that are to come." (John 16:13)

Think about your current prayer life. How dependent are you on the power of the Holy Spirit in prayer? Have you learned how to listen to the voice of the Holy Spirit guiding you? Are you more in tune with God's agenda or your personal agenda when you pray? Christian prayer must be dependent on the Holy Spirit.

Jesus said to him, "I am the way, and the truth, and the life. No one comes to the Father except through me." (John 14:6)

Now that we have discussed what Christian prayer is as it relates to the Trinity, let's take a closer look at how we direct how prayer to the triune God. Christian prayer is *to the Father, through the Son, in the power of the Holy Spirit*. That is a mouthful and another important distinction of Christian prayer. Let's break down this definition briefly. First, Christian prayer is to "Our Father." (See Luke 11:1-4.) The Greek word used here is *Abba*, which we might interpret as Papa or Daddy. This term is both affectionate and familial. In the Jewish tradition, only children called their father *Abba*. Do you recognize how controversial it was for Jesus to suggest to that Jewish audience that the members of his family would call God *Abba*? How do you refer to God in prayer? Depending on our past, many of us may struggle with intimate, endearing terms like *Abba* to refer to God. But clearly, the Lord's Prayer instructs us to approach God that way. Jesus taught us to pray, "Father, hallowed be your name."

Second, Christian prayer is *through the Son*. It may be a new idea for you to consider that Christian prayer comes only through Jesus, but John 14:6 makes this truth clear. Prayer that attempts to come to God without a relationship with Jesus is, by this definition, not Christian prayer. We pray to a holy God, through his Son, so that we will be transformed into God's likeness, and so come to know him. Have you emphasized your relationship with God through Jesus in prayer?

Third, we often struggle to pray, but God understands and has sent us a Helper, the Holy Spirit. (Christian prayer is by the one Spirit.) Jesus sent the Holy Spirit as the Father sent the

Son—to reveal himself to mankind. Romans 8:26-27 is one scripture of many that underscores the role of the Holy Spirit in prayer.

Likewise the Spirit helps us in our weakness; for we do not know how to pray as we ought, but that very Spirit intercedes with sighs too deep for words. And God, who searches the heart, knows what is the mind of the Spirit, because the Spirit intercedes for the saints according to the will of God. (Romans 8:26-27)

Do you want to learn how to pray according to the will of God 100 percent of the time? Scripture gives us a clear directive to accomplish praying God's will. We must begin with the understanding that in our weakness, our own human understanding, we do not know how to pray as we ought. Instead, the Holy Spirit must empower and direct our prayers. Then, and I would suggest only then, will our prayers be according to the will of God.

Unfortunately, many of us are *bi-nitarians*. Our theology of God the Father and God the Son is relatively clear. However, God the Holy Spirit remains a mystery. We may have missed the importance of the third person of the Trinity in our understanding of prayer. Consider your current prayer life? How dependent on the Holy Spirit are you? What do you need to do to grow in your understanding of the person and work of the Holy Spirit?

Our relationship with God is made possible through the Spirit, who guides us in our prayers and shows us how to pray through Jesus to the Father. We need to embrace this work of the Holy Spirit in prayer. As we learn how to appropriate the power of the Holy Spirit, our prayer life will mature and become increasingly powerful and effective.

Prayer is communication. I did not personally experience the truth of that statement early in my prayer life. As much as I've learned about the importance of listening in prayer, I still consider listening my weakest area of prayer and the place where I want to grow the most. I understand more fully now that God speaks in a variety of ways, and I rejoice that I hear God's voice more clearly with each passing day. Nevertheless, the cry of my heart remains, "More God." Today, I am much more likely to end a season of prayer with the question, "What did God say?" I'm learning to embrace seasons of silence so that God and I can truly have a conversation.

Talking to God is still a growing understanding for me. However, I vividly remember a time in my prayer life when being what I term "emotionally real" was very difficult for me. I held God at arms length. I never talked to God when I was angry, when I was disappointed, or when I experienced other negative emotions. It has been a real step of growth for me to bring my emotions to the Lord in prayer.

Prayer has become an important aspect of my Christian walk, one area where I am open to growth in my relationship with Christ. But that was not always true. I remember a time when I would have described my prayer life like this: *I need, I want. I need, I want. They need, they want. They need, they want.* Honestly, I thought almost entirely about a long list of requests when I went to God in prayer. Fostering a love relationship with God was probably the furthest thing from my mind at that point in my prayer life. By God's grace, my prayer life changed with time. I came to understand the need for fostering my love relationship with God through strong teaching on worship and adoration. Currently, I spend much less time on my *laundry list* of needs, and much more time just enjoying God's presence in prayer.

Likewise, my prayer life changed when I understood more about Jesus' role as intercessor. Do you ever worry about saying a prayer just right in hopes that God will hear and answer? I did! Legalism and fear were my partners in prayer. Knowing the truth of God's Word, that Jesus ever lives to make intercession for the saints, brought me great freedom and healing. No longer do I strive to form my prayers according to some unrealistic expectations. I've learned to speak to God freely from my heart. I also began to inquire of the Lord more often. I listen, really listen, much more. Prayer is no longer a duty or a discipline I engage in out of fear. It has become a delight.

My prayer life changed with greater understanding of each aspect of the Trinity. However, it changed most dramatically when I came to understand the person and work of the Holy Spirit. Have you ever had God put his finger on your life through the Word? That was my experience. God used Matthew 22:29 to dramatically change my prayer life.

Jesus answered them, "You are wrong, because you know neither the scriptures nor the power of God." (Matthew 22:29)

I remember the experience well! It was a low point in my life when I was asking God many questions about my faith. I was struggling to trust in a Father who heard and answered prayer. God said, "Margie, you are in error because you do not know the scriptures, and you do not know the power of my Holy Spirit." I was touched at the core of my being, and that incident sent me on a profound journey. My journey included intensive Bible reading and memorization. I made a choice to hide God's Word in my heart. That decision changed my life. In addition, I searched God's Word for a deeper understanding of the Holy Spirit. God enriched my life with Spirit-filled people that led and encouraged me on my journey. This wonderful journey with the Holy Spirit continues today.

Questions for Personal Reflection

1. How important is listening in your communication with God in prayer?
2. Reflect on the variety of ways that God speaks to you. What was the last thing God said to you?
3. Jesus is our mediator in prayer. Has your view of Jesus' role in prayer changed?
4. Is your prayer life a duty, a discipline, or a delight?

Activities for Small Groups

1. Thank God for the gift of the Holy Spirit to empower your prayer life.
2. Pray for one another according to Romans 8:26-27. Here's a sample prayer: "Holy Spirit, help (insert name) to know her/his own weakness in prayer. Empower (insert name)'s prayer life. May (insert name) experience the Holy Spirit's direction in prayer so that (insert name) knows your heart and prays according to your will."

Lessons from the Prayer Life of Jesus

Who do you look to as a model for growing in your personal prayer life? Do you have someone that taught you the importance of prayer? If you do, you are truly blessed. However, there is one in the scriptures who is our best model of communication with the Father. His name is Jesus! All of us can grow as we look at the prayer life of Jesus. His prayer life is a model for our personal prayer life. Why did Jesus pray, what did Jesus pray, and when did Jesus pray are questions we will answer from the scriptures. Our purpose is to apply these lessons to our own lives and grow in our ability to pray as Jesus did.

CHAPTER THREE

Why Did Jesus Pray?

W hy did Jesus pray? Asking that question is somewhat like asking why is rain wet? Jesus prayed because it was in his nature and character to do so. Jesus was made for communication with the Father. He had experienced the power and presence of Father God in Heaven. When he came to earth, Jesus understood the absolute importance of maintaining communication with God at all times. We need to see that the reasons Jesus prayed are the same reasons we need to pray. In this chapter we will look briefly at five scriptural reasons why Jesus prayed.

In the morning, while it was still very dark, he got up and went out to a deserted place, and there he prayed. (Mark 1:35)

First, Jesus prayed because he needed time alone with the Father. Mark 1:35 highlights this truth. Jesus chose a deserted place because of the importance he placed on being alone with the Father to pray. Jesus made this time alone a priority. Before anything else could crowd into his day, Jesus chose a personal prayer time.

But now more than ever the word about Jesus spread abroad; many crowds would gather to hear him and to be cured of their diseases. But he would withdraw to deserted places and pray. (Luke 5:15-16)

Luke 5:15-16 also shows us that Jesus often withdrew to lonely places and prayed. Jesus had a pattern of time away, not just an occasional withdrawal from the demands of life. Jesus' life and ministry was extremely demanding, but nowhere do we see Jesus making excuses for not spending time with his Father. How about you and me?

What helps can we offer for those who struggle to find time alone with God? Consider these ideas. Choose a consistent time and place. If you know that you have a quiet place of retreat for prayer, your time with the Lord can be more inviting and meaningful. In addition, build times of Sabbath or personal retreat into your schedule. Take time, perhaps once a quarter, when you know you can break out of your everyday routine and spend concentrated time in prayer and Bible reading. This practice can really accelerate your growth in prayer and give you new insights from the Lord. Give yourself permission to have regular times of retreat for prayer.

Perhaps most important, receive God's grace for your failures. Even with the best of intentions, you may not be able to find a place and space for prayer 100 percent of the time. When you get off track, ask God's forgiveness, receive his grace, and start fresh again.

Remember that the Holy Spirit works within each of us to create change. We don't operate on the world's philosophy of, "try a little harder, do a little better." Instead, we submit and surrender to the Holy Spirit daily. Make your time alone with God a priority in prayer. Ask God to carve out time each day for you to meet with him. Then, watch how God answers that prayer!

Jesus said to them, "Very truly, I tell you, the Son can do nothing on his own, but only what he sees the Father doing; for whatever the Father does, the Son does likewise." (John 5:19)

Jesus also prayed because he needed to hear from God for guidance. John 5:19 gives us a clear scriptural indication for why Jesus prayed. What an exciting verse. Clearly, Jesus modeled doing nothing on his own. He practiced prayerful dependence on the Father. He did and said only those things that came from the Father. And, by the power of the Holy Spirit, so can we!

What helps can we offer for those who struggle to hear from and receive God's guidance? Be patient. So often, God's timetable is not ours. We must learn to wait on the Lord in silence. This silence includes more than absence of talking. It includes learning to silence our mind, our will, and our emotions that often hinder us from hearing from the Lord. Recognize that God speaks in a variety of ways and desires to guide us more than we can know or understand.

We must not fall prey to comparison with others regarding prayer. Often comparison breeds disappointment or discouragement. We may even give up our quest to grow in our ability to hear from God. One person's testimony of an answer to prayer, though exciting and spectacular, should never derail us from hearing the still small voice of the Spirit.

Also, we must be honest with God about our feelings. When we are feeling frustrated, impatient, even angry we should talk to God about those feelings. Feelings are God-given, and they are good. But God never meant for us to base our walk with the Lord entirely on our feelings.

Now during those days he went out to the mountain to pray; and he spent the night in prayer to God. And when day came, he called his disciples and chose twelve of them, whom he also named apostles: Simon, whom he named Peter, and his brother Andrew, and James, and John, and Philip, and Bartholomew, and Matthew, and Thomas, and James son of Alphaeus, and Simon, who was called the Zealot, and Judas son of James, and Judas Iscariot, who became a traitor. (Luke 6:12-16)

Third, why did Jesus pray? Jesus needed wisdom to teach the disciples. Before every ministry decision, Jesus spent time in prayer. Luke 6:12 is one example. This is a pattern that all of us can follow. How much time is enough time in prayer? I've asked myself that question often. In Jesus' example of choosing the apostles, it seems evident that Jesus prayed until the answer came. He did not resort to making a decision and then asking God to bless it. He waited on the Father's guidance and then he moved out in confidence.

Fourth, Jesus prayed because he needed God's strength in temptation. One classic example is Matthew 4:1-11. When faced with Satan's attack, Jesus modeled prayer and fasting in the wilderness. How does the enemy attack you? Have you experienced the temptation to hold grudges, to gossip? Are you plagued with unhealthy thoughts, low self-esteem, or fear of failure? When the enemy comes in like a flood, we need to know

God will give us strength for every temptation. When the enemy attempts to cause confusion and doubt, plagues us with questions about our ministry, or hinders us with fear for our future, we need to follow Jesus' example of steadfast prayer. Jesus stayed true to the ministry the Father had laid out for him rather than succumbing to the will of the crowds. Will you do likewise?

Now when Jesus heard this, he withdrew from there in a boat to a deserted place by himself. (Matthew 14:13)

Last, Jesus prayed because he needed to deal with personal grief and pain. The story of the beheading of John the Baptist from Matthew 14:13 is a good example. Jesus sought out time alone with the Father when he heard the news of John's death. We can learn from Jesus' example that God wants to hear about our grief and pain. Having friends who can walk with us through difficult times is comforting and important. But having Jesus, our best friend, who understands perfectly our pain and grief can be so much more important. Learning to come to Jesus in prayer for even the most difficult circumstances of our lives can be a real step of growth for us.

For all the reasons Jesus prayed, I want to learn to go to God in prayer. By God's grace, I'm determined to follow Jesus' example and have made John 5:19 one of my life verses. More and more, I'm learning prayerful dependence on the Lord. I'm learning to inquire of the Lord and recognize that apart from him I can do no good thing. Do I still struggle to have consistent personal time alone with God? Definitely. However, now I receive God's grace for my failures and am growing in that area. I've cried out to God to help me be consistent in prayer, and I see God's answer manifesting in my life. One constant setting for me is the *prayer chair* in my bedroom. I know that I can pray anywhere, but I find it easier to drop into prayer there than many other places—perhaps because I have prayed there so often.

Do I still struggle to get guidance from God at times? Of course! I believe I struggle mostly with waiting to hear. I can be so impatient and shortsighted. However, if I'm honest, the real problem is sometimes I don't like what I hear. God's guidance is not always easy or agreeable to my nature. Mostly, I'm learning the importance of obedience to the guidance I do receive from the Lord. With obedience always comes God's blessing. When I am obedient to the simplest guidance of the Lord, I am better able to hear God's Word to me the next time.

I also need God's strength in temptation. As I evaluate my walk with the Lord, perhaps the desire for approval of others and the fear of rejection or abandonment hinders me as much as any other temptations. I've come to see that these fears in my life lead to compromise. I will often question, "Did I hear from God?" Recognizing the temptation is a major step in the victory over my fear. Among the many possible temptations, I see the temptation to be judgmental or controlling often in my life. I'm learning to run to God in prayer at those times. A simple breath prayer saying, "Help me, Lord" often helps me find the immediate victory I seek.

Jesus used the truth of the Word to overcome Satan, God's enemy and ours. I'm learning how to defeat the lies of the enemy by saturating my prayers with God's Word. When faced with Satan's attacks, Jesus answered, "It is written." More and more, I'm learning the victory of declaring the promises of the Word in prayer.

Questions for Personal Reflection

1. How often do you spend quiet time alone with God? What steps can you take to make this a pattern in your life?

2. Do you have a pressing need to hear from God today? Seek God in prayer for his wisdom or guidance. Place your confidence in God to answer.

3. Take stock of your prayer life. What is a current temptation you are facing? Think about the last time you yielded to this temptation. What might you do differently the next time? Pray and ask God to show you how to overcome this enticement.

4. Are you facing personal grief or pain? Take it to the Lord in prayer. Receive his comfort and expect a manifestation of God's abundant love for you.

Activities for Small Groups

1. Thank God for Jesus' example of prayer and consistent communication with the Father.

2. Pray for one another. If your group members are experiencing temptations, trials, or grief and pain, spend time praying for these concerns.

CHAPTER FOUR

What Did Jesus Pray?

In the course of the three years Jesus spent in ministry and close association with his disciples, I have no doubt they witnessed Jesus praying many times. However, only a few of those instances are recorded in scripture. Many times all the Bible says is "Jesus prayed," and we are left to our own inferences about what Jesus might have prayed. In this section, we will look closely at two specific prayers of Jesus. These prayers are in John 12:23-28 and Matthew 26: 36-46. Jesus remains our best model of communication with the Father, and we should look to his prayers as examples to follow.

"Father, glorify your name." Then a voice came from heaven, "I have glorified it, and I will glorify it again." (John 12:28)

John 12:23-28 records Jesus' own prediction of his death and these simple but profound words of prayer, "Father, glorify your name." Using the analogy of a kernel of wheat, Jesus explains the importance of his death. Jesus also teaches us that those who love this temporal life more than God's kingdom purposes will lose their life for eternity.

"Father, glorify your name." Have you ever prayed those words? Would your prayers change if your ultimate purpose were to glorify the Father? If we were to follow Jesus' example, our prayers for our workplace, or family life, or church would center on God's will and lifting up Jesus rather than our own personal thoughts and desires.

How is the Father glorified in our personal prayer life? When we seek God's kingdom priorities—like salvation of the lost, care for the poor, healing for the hurting—God is glorified. When we understand that we were created to bring God pleasure and not the reverse, God is glorified. When our prayers are filled with listening for what God wants, God is glorified. When God's agenda is more important than our own wants and desires, God is glorified. When our prayers are more *other-centered* than *me-centered*, God is glorified. When we rise up from prayer and obey what God has charged us to do, God is glorified.

Jesus' simple prayer, "Father, glorify your name," will always overcome our own will and break the stronghold of selfishness in prayer. Pray it often.

And going a little farther, he threw himself on the ground and prayed, "My Father, if it is possible, let this cup pass from me; yet not what I want but what you want." (Matthew 26:39)

Matthew 26:36-46 gives us another specific example of what Jesus prayed. While in the Garden of Gethsemane, on the night of his betrayal and arrest, Jesus prayed, "yet not what I want but what you want." Have you ever prayed those words? If you were to follow Jesus' example, would your personal prayer life change? In order to pray this prayer with sincerity, our lives must be totally committed and surrendered to the Lord. We cannot take this need for surrender lightly.

Selfishness in prayer shows itself when most of our prayers revolve around asking God for personal needs. The *I need, I want* prayers have a place in personal prayer. God absolutely cares about our personal needs and wants us to talk to him about those needs; however, balance is the key. When we pray for our own personal needs at the exclusion of the needs of others, we can be out of balance.

In the days of his flesh, Jesus offered up prayers and supplications, with loud cries and tears, to the one who was able to save him from death, and he was heard because of his reverent submission. (Hebrews 5:7)

Hebrews 5:7 adds an important element to our understanding of submitting to God's will in prayer. Jesus was heard because of his reverent submission. Because of the truth of this scripture, we see our need to learn submission to God in every area of our life if our prayers are going to be effective. Although it may be challenging to live in submission to God, the rewards to our prayer life seem obvious.

I am learning submission to God balanced with the need to be emotionally real in prayer. Those are two different but equally important aspects of prayer. We can express our true feelings to God knowing that he is able and willing to deal with our honesty. That was a progressive understanding for me. There was definitely a time in my prayer life when I held God at arm's length and never talked to him when I was angry, hurting, or disappointed. But each of us must also learn reverent submission to God. Like many of us, my deepest lessons in prayer came primarily during the greatest trials of my life.

Praying Jesus' prayer, "yet not what I want but what you want," is becoming a pattern in my prayer life. I'm learning to pray this prayer daily to develop an attitude of consistent submission to the will of God. We cannot wait to pray this way until trials come. If we wait until catastrophe strikes, we may be so caught up in the emotion of the circumstances that we are unable to pray as Jesus did. We need to set our heart on dying to self every day. Before trials come—and they will come—it is best to learn these lessons about selfishness and submission to God in prayer. Then I am prepared for what lay ahead because I have already determined in my heart to pray, "Father, glorify your name," and "yet not what I want, but what you want."

Have you ever asked God in prayer, "Father, what is your will for me? What do you want for me?" In response to those questions in prayer, God clearly spoke "forgiveness" to my heart. My prayer life changed for the better and prepared me for what lay ahead when I made a decision to walk in forgiveness—regardless of the circumstances. Even before the offenses come, I can make a conscious choice to forgive. Unforgiveness really is a trap of the enemy. We must learn not to take the bait. That temptation remains very real for all of us, but more and more I am choosing a lifestyle of forgiveness. Without question, walking in forgiveness is what God wants for us.

Praying not what I want but what you want became very important during times of trial with my children. Both of my sons are grown now, but my eldest son had a problem with drugs and alcohol during his teens. I'm grateful that God was teaching me these lessons about submission to God before the magnitude of my son's problems affected our family. Through the pain, I learned to pray, "God, you know best. You love my children even more than I possibly could. Have your way!" Because I was becoming more conscious of praying God's kingdom priorities at this time, I understood that God's highest priority is that my children would walk with Christ. Recognizing God's unfailing love for my children, I was able to pray, "God, whatever it takes." I believe that is a very bold prayer. Thankfully, God heard those earnest prayers of surrender and intercession for my children and moved mightily.

Questions for Personal Reflection

1. Where are you currently learning submission to God in prayer?
2. Are you emotionally real in prayer? Give a current example.
3. Do you struggle with selfishness in prayer? How is God teaching you to overcome this weakness?
4. How would your prayer life change if you consistently prayed, "not what I want but what you want"?

Activities for Small Groups

1. Thank God for Jesus' life, death, and resurrection. Spend some time praising God for being your "Suffering Servant" (Isaiah 53).
2. Pray for one another to walk in submission to God's will—to glorify the Father.
3. Spend some time in silence, practicing your listening skills in prayer.
4. Pray Colossians 3:17 for a partner. Here's a sample prayer: "Heavenly Father, enable (insert name) to be full of the Holy Spirit. May (insert name) speak, act, and live submitted to your will, Lord, bringing glory to your name."

CHAPTER FIVE

When Did Jesus Pray?

Once again, we can learn much from Jesus' pattern of prayer. Jesus prayed alone—consistently and purposely. But he also prayed with others. The scriptures give us examples of the importance Jesus placed on having others in prayer with him. Both important aspects of Jesus' prayer life should be reflected in our prayer life.

Immediately [Jesus] made the disciples get into the boat and go on ahead to the other side, while he dismissed the crowds. After he had dismissed the crowds, he went up on a mountain by himself to pray. When evening came, he was there alone, but by this time the boat, battered by the waves, was far from the land, for the wind was against them. (Matthew 14:22-24)

Matthew 14:22-24 gives us a good example of Jesus' time alone in prayer. Put this scripture in context. Just prior to this time of prayer, Jesus had fed 5000 families. Then he went up on the mountainside to pray. Early in the morning, Jesus walks on water and comes to his disciples in the boat. Peter begins to walk on water out to Jesus but is overcome by fear. When they got into the boat together, the wind ceased and all was calm. Together they crossed over to Gennesaret and Jesus immediately resumes his healing ministry.

Jesus' solitary time in prayer comes in the midst of hectic, demanding times of ministry. His precious times alone with his Father are what fueled his ministry and empowered him to stay true to his mission to preach, teach, and heal.

Jesus also modeled praying with others. Luke 9:28-29 is a good example. Jesus invited Peter, James, and John to join him in prayer on a mountain. Because they joined him, these disciples witnessed the transfiguration of Christ.

How important is praying with others in your personal prayer life? Do you seek out opportunities to pray with a prayer partner or a small group of believers? Some of us are hindered in our understanding of why we should pray with others. We haven't made corporate prayer a priority, perhaps, because we are afraid to pray out loud in a group. Why do we pray out loud? How do we pray in agreement with others? These are important questions.

"Again, truly I tell you, if two of you agree on earth about anything you ask, it will be done for you by my Father in heaven. For where two or three are gathered in my name, I am there among them." (Matthew 18:19-20)

Matthew 18:19-20 is often called the prayer of agreement. It teaches us the importance of praying together. Simply put, in order to agree with a partner in prayer, we must be able to hear that prayer. That is why we pray out loud. When we're listening to another person in prayer, we are not to be judging that person's prayer. We're not to be thinking about how we could have said the prayer better or differently. Instead, our purpose is to be in agreement. Our heart and our lips should be saying, "Yes, God. I agree." There is great power in praying in agreement, but that is only one reason why we should pray together.

Praying together increases our protection from the enemy and gives us power over his attacks.

> *You shall give chase to your enemies, and they shall fall before you by the sword. Five of you shall give chase to a hundred, and a hundred of you shall give chase to ten thousand; your enemies shall fall before you by the sword.* (Leviticus 26:7-8)

Leviticus 26:7-8 and Ecclesiastes 4:12 speak of the multiplied power of praying as a group. When we pray together in unity and incorporate praying the promises of the Word of God, our prayers are powerful and effective against the enemy. Praying together also offers us much needed support for discouragement. Consider Ecclesiastes 4:9-10. God meant for us to bear one another's burdens and help each other in times of trouble. We often find the strength to overcome through the prayer support of others.

> *Two are better than one, because they have a good reward for their toil. For if they fall, one will lift up the other; but woe to one who is alone and falls and does not have another to help.* (Ecclesiastes 4:9-10)

There are other benefits to praying together. Here are a few good reasons for each of us to make corporate prayer a priority. There is accountability and wisdom from a group. Often, God will provide confirmation of guidance and an increased sense of hearing from God. Without question, the gifts of the Holy Spirit were given to the body of Christ. None of us will manifest all of the gifts individually. But together we will always experience more of the gifts of the Spirit.

Jesus prayed alone, and he prayed with others. I want that to be my experience as well. Jesus needed solitary time in the midst of hectic ministry. So do I! Call it what you want, perhaps daily quiet time, these precious moments alone with God are the secret of a life dedicated to Jesus. I'm learning to make time alone with God the foundation for all other aspects of my life. When I was first beginning to understand the importance of praying alone, I made a covenant with God. I started small. I asked God to help me give him the first seven minutes of my day. From those small beginnings God has brought multiplied growth.

I also love to pray with others. If given the opportunity to pray with others, I want to be there. I find I see more of God in corporate prayer. For example, God's wisdom and guidance seem easier in corporate prayer. As my prayer partner and I pray together about different aspects of a problem, there is increased depth in prayer—I hear God more clearly and receive confirmation of his guidance. (Different individuals bring unique perspectives of God's direction.) My faith is stirred, and I love coming into agreement with others in prayer.

Balance is the key to a healthy prayer life. I want to balance personal prayer and corporate prayer. I think of it like an iceberg. Only ten percent of an iceberg is visible, while the other ninety percent is hidden below the surface. That is my personal goal. I desire to make only ten percent of my prayer life visible. The other ninety percent is alone with God in my prayer closet. I believe God has greatly blessed this desire to be balanced in prayer.

When I first began to pray with others, I had to overcome the fear that others would judge my prayers. I was hesitant to pray out loud because I was usually praying with more mature believers and thought their prayers were more eloquent than mine. God rescued me from comparison with these words, "Comparison breeds death." I understood from this encounter with God that my corporate prayer life would die unless I overcame this fear of comparison. God's healing came as I took this need to the Lord in prayer. I gained a real love of praying with others in a group.

Comparing my prayer life with others was only one hindrance. I also was guilty of praying corporately to seek the approval of others. When God made me aware of my hidden needs in prayer, I again sought his healing. Whatever hindrances God may highlight as you strive to grow in corporate prayer, be assured that he alone is the source of healing.

Getting started in corporate prayer was not easy. One help I can offer is to pray out loud in your personal quiet times. Learning to hear your own voice in prayer privately will help you make the jump to praying out loud corporately. An added benefit I discovered was that praying out loud really helps me stay focused. My mind is much less likely to wander when I am praying softly out loud, even in my daily quiet time with the Lord. Also, I love having a prayer partner. Starting with one trusted person to pray with consistently is an encouragement all of us need. If you do not have a prayer partner, I recommend that you ask God to provide one.

Next, we can progress to praying with a small group. My experience with small group prayer has been very rewarding. As a group we experimented with different styles of prayer and a variety of tools to enhance our experience. Together we agreed that silence is not bad, which is an important consideration. Many of us are afraid of silence in prayer and will fill the void with something. Anything! If you want to grow in corporate prayer, start by valuing times of silence. Next, practice praying over one topic at a time and giving each member of the group an opportunity to pray for that need. Learning to appreciate, welcome, and encourage the prayers of all the members of the group may take some time, but it is worth the effort.

Questions for Personal Reflection

1. What balance do you see in your prayer life between personal prayer and corporate prayer?
2. Where have you experienced the prayer support of others?
3. How important are the prayers of others when you face the attacks of the enemy?

Activities for Small Groups

1. Pray sentence prayers expressing praise for one attribute of God's character for which you are thankful. Example: "I praise you God for your faithfulness."
2. Allow members of the group to briefly share about a prayer request for themselves or someone else. Pray together, lifting these needs to the Lord. Stay with sentence prayers, allowing everyone to participate.

Tools for Personal Prayer

Think about the tools you have around your home. Most of us have hammers, screwdrivers, or saws readily available. Each of these tools has a specific purpose. We could probably use a wrench to pound in a nail, but it is not the best tool for that project. Having the appropriate tools available in our toolbox makes building and repair projects easier to accomplish.

The same is true in the spiritual realm. Tools are needed to build our personal prayer life. Each of the next ten chapters will present a helpful tool to build a lifestyle of prayer. Prayer has been defined as a relationship with Christ; therefore, our prayer tools are used to build that relationship. Never look at these tools as one more thing I *have* to do. Beware of legalism. Nobody uses all ten of these tools every day. The joy of walking with the Spirit is that he will be our guide. When the Holy Spirit says, "It's time to fast, or you should journal today," the builder should have those tools for personal prayer ready.

CHAPTER SIX

Fasting

Fasting is a wonderful tool to draw us into a closer relationship with Christ. We should always fast under the guidance of the Holy Spirit. Be led by the Spirit for the type and duration of your fast.

Fasting could be defined as abstinence from all or certain foods. Fasting is not therapeutic dieting. In the scriptures, fasting is always combined with seeking God in prayer. Fasting has less to do with food and more to do with seeking God in a focused manner.

The definition of fasting can also include abstinence from certain activities in order to seek God in prayer. What absorbs your time? Television, the Internet, hobbies, computer games, and shopping may all be examples of activities to abstain from in order to spend more time in prayer. For medical reasons, some of us may be unable to fast from food, but we can all fast from activities in order to seek God in prayer.

---

*"And whenever you fast, do not look dismal, like the hyp-
ocrites, for they disfigure their faces so as to show others
that they are fasting. Truly I tell you, they have received
their reward. But when you fast, put oil on your head and
wash your face, so that your fasting may be seen not by
others but by your Father who sees in secret; and your
Father will reward you."* (Matthew 6:16-18)

The Bible has much to say about fasting. Consider Matthew
6:16-18. The words "when you fast" indicate that followers of
Christ will fast. When done in accordance with God's Word, our
fast is rewarded with deeper intimacy with the Father and
increased effectiveness in prayer.

There are a variety of reasons for fasting. According to
Zechariah 7:5, we fast unto the Lord. We need to ask God to sift
our motives for fasting. God's question in Zechariah is a good
one for us. "When you fasted and lamented, was it for me that
you fasted?"

Personal sanctity is a second good reason to include fasting
with prayer. Psalm 69:10 says, "When I humbled my soul with
fasting." As we pursue personal holiness, fasting will humble us.
With humility will come greater spiritual power and a release of
spiritual gifts.

A third good reason is the discipline of fasting helps to put
our lives in divine order. We are created with a body, a soul, and
a spirit. God's plan is that the spirit would be in control over the
body or the soul. Our spirit should take precedence over our
body or our mind, our will and our emotions. Fasting often shows
us the ways that the body is not submitted to the spirit. When we
begin to fast, our body will cry out for food. Likewise, our *soulish*
nature screams out for attention during times of fasting. Our
mind, our will, and our emotions can hinder our attempts to fast.

It takes discipline and the empowerment of the Holy Spirit to fast. During prayer ask God to show you any ways your soul or your body is not submitted to the Holy Spirit.

Is not this the fast that I choose: to loose the bonds of injustice, to undo the thongs of the yoke, to let the oppressed go free, and to break every yoke. (Isaiah 58:6)

Fourth, fasting is an effective tool when praying to free the captives. Consider Isaiah 58:6-7. There are times when an urgent need calls for fasting. If you are interceding for loved ones who are oppressed by the enemy, fasting can be an effective addition to spiritual warfare prayers.

Do you need to hear from God? Is there a circumstance in your life where you are actively seeking God's guidance? If so, consider this last reason for fasting—to receive revelation. Many times in scripture God poured out revelation knowledge to those who were earnestly seeking him in prayer and fasting. The prophet Daniel is a good example. Daniel was praying about the desolation of Jerusalem that he perceived would last seventy years (Daniel 9:2-3). In response to Daniel's prayers, God sent the angel Gabriel to give him "wisdom and understanding" of things to come (verses 21-22). Our Lord can do the same for each one who seeks him in prayer and fasting.

In addition to reasons for fasting, there are various types of fasts. Here is a brief description of some you may consider. Before fasting from food, it is recommended that you seek the advice of a medical professional. Certain medical conditions may preclude your fasting from food.

A normal fast means abstaining from all food, solid or liquid, but not water. The timeframe for a normal fast may vary. As a beginner you may choose to fast for one meal or one day. You can then extend the period of fasting as the Lord leads.

An absolute fast means abstaining from drinking as well as eating. The timeframe for an absolute fast can also vary; however, this fast would normally be limited to three days. Since the body can go long periods without food, but only for a very short time without water, a duration of longer than three days might prove to be physically harmful.

There are instances in scripture of a supernatural fast. There are examples from Moses' life (Deuteronomy 9:9, 17-18) when God provided supernatural help so that he could go many days without food or water. Supernatural fasts are obviously only accomplished under the direction of the Holy Spirit.

At that time I, Daniel, had been mourning for three weeks. I had eaten no rich food, no meat or wine had entered my mouth, and I had not anointed myself at all, for the full three weeks. (Daniel 10:2-3)

Many times God may call us to a partial fast which means the restriction of our diet rather than complete abstention from food. For example, Daniel limited his diet choosing to abstain from all rich food, meat, and wine in Daniel 10:2-3. John Wesley, the founder of Methodism, adopted a bread diet during his early days in Georgia (Wesley's Journal, Volume 1). He lived exclusively on dry bread and water for a time. That's another example of a more restrictive partial fast.

Sanctify a fast; call a solemn assembly. (Joel 2:15)

Public fasts may also become part of our prayer experience. These are organized, intentional periods of abstaining from food with others who are also seeking the Lord in prayer. Joel 2:15 is a scriptural example of a public corporate fast. Like Joel's solemn assembly, there may be times when spiritual leaders will call the body of Christ to a specific time of corporate fasting and prayer. For example, churches may fast together during times of seeking God's wisdom for an evangelistic effort, a building project, or transition in leadership.

John Wesley gives us an example of a regular fast. In the second and third centuries after Christ, the Wednesday and Friday of each week became recognized as fast days, and John Wesley revived this custom among the early Methodists.

In addition, Wesley charged his preachers with nineteen questions to affirm their calling and commitment to the Lord before commissioning them. Question 16 affirms the spiritual discipline of fasting as a means of growing in holiness of heart and life. It asks, "Will you recommend fasting and abstinence, both by precept and example?" Under Wesley, Methodist pastors were expected to teach fasting to their congregations by biblical instruction and by their example.

I still consider myself a beginner in the area of fasting. But I pursue fasting because I want my prayers to be effective. Sometimes my fasting is only for one meal as I seek the Lord in prayer. I consider fasting mostly as a means to humble myself before God. Dying to self and allowing the Spirit to be in control is important to me. The fact is that our bodies and the appetites of the flesh in this world can govern us. Fasting helps break the rhythm of life in our culture that revolves around eating.

As an intercessor, I am called by God to stand in the gap and pray for the lost, the oppressed, and those in bondage. Some of my own family members fall into these categories. Fasting combined with spiritual warfare prayers are a part of my intercession

for others. In addition, I believe my "spiritual ears" are more sen-
sitive to the voice of the Holy Spirit when I am fasting. Receiving
God's wisdom and direction in prayer increases the effectiveness
of my prayers.

When first called to fast, I started slowly and followed the
guidance of the Holy Spirit. That's good advice for each of us.
Perhaps my best example of fasting comes from a team teaching
event in a local church. The team experienced the benefits of
being recipients of much prayer and fasting. I appreciated the
way the pastor introduced fasting to his congregation as a means
of preparing for the renewal event in his local church. He simply
announced to his congregation that he was led by the Spirit to
engage in a thirty-day normal fast. During that time he would
drink only water. He combined seasons of prayer with fasting and
opened the church every morning at 6:00 a.m., inviting others to
join him in prayer as the Lord led. There was no legalism or coer-
cion to participate. He simply led by example. During this time,
many others in the congregation fasted from activities in order to
spend extra time in prayer. I remember one man gave up golf.
Several engaged in a partial fast. I remember one person who
gave up eating cookies. During the time of fasting and prayer, the
team members received almost daily e-mails from the pastor. We
were encouraged when we heard about miracles of healing,
restoration in families, and revelation from the Lord during this
time. When we arrived at the church for the weekend event, the
team was amazed at the power and presence of the Lord in the
church. Team members knew that their teaching and testimony
were secondary to the prayer and fasting that had preceded the
event. Fasting and prayer prepared the way for a powerful move
of renewal in the church.

Questions for Personal Reflection

1. Is God leading you to fast?
2. What type of fast should you consider?
3. Reflect on this statement: A true fast occurs when we abstain for the purpose of seeking God in a more focused manner.
4. Is there a situation in your local church that calls for a public corporate fast?

Activities for Small Groups

1. Share personal experiences related to fasting in your small group.
2. Pray for each other for guidance in applying fasting to your prayer life.

CHAPTER SEVEN

Listening

Listening means, "to give ear, to hearken, to give heed." For our purposes, listening in prayer means learning to hear the voice of the Lord. One helpful amplified definition says that hearing involves the physical act of hearing with our ears, the mental activity of processing the sounds and understanding what is said in our minds, followed by the action of obeying what was heard in our lives. Hearing, understanding, and obeying is a full definition of listening. Since prayer is a conversation with God, listening is an important tool in our prayer life.

As we endeavor to listen in prayer, we need to acknowledge the wide variety of ways that God speaks to us. One primary means of communication with God is through the scriptures. As we read God's Word, the Holy Spirit will speak directly to our lives. The written word comes alive for our individual circumstances, and we know that God has spoken to us. What was the last thing God spoke to you through the Word? Did you obey?

God will also speak to us through our thoughts. As we're asking God a question, for example, a thought may come into our mind that answers our need. Remember that not every thought we have is a godly thought. So the process of listening always involves discernment. Is what we're hearing from the Lord or just our own thought process? Learning to hear the voice of the Lord is always spiritually discerned. But the good news is God wants to speak to us and will teach us how to listen more effectively and mature in discernment.

God also speaks to us through visions and dreams or spiritual pictures that give us guidance and wisdom. Again, spiritual discernment must be at work. Often having a trusted Christian friend as a prayer partner will help us know how to interpret and apply the visions and dreams we see and hear from the Lord.

God loves to speak through other people. There are times we can gain godly wisdom and discernment from spiritual leaders and friends. Their counsel may be one way we hear from God. However, we also need to learn how to test what we hear. God will keep us from being led astray if we always consult God regarding the advice of others.

God will also speak through circumstances. Some people use *open doors* and *closed doors* to determine guidance from the Lord. God does communicate that way. When seeking God's guidance, we can look for open doors of opportunity as one means that God speaks to us. However, it is often wise to consider circumstances last. Instead, get your final *go ahead* from scripture and wise counsel.

"When he has brought out all his own, he goes ahead of them, and the sheep follow him because they know his voice. They will not follow a stranger, but they will run from him because they do not know the voice of strangers." (John 10:4-5)

Understanding what the Bible says about listening is important. Consider John 10:4-5. This is a wonderful promise from Jesus, the Good Shepherd. We are his sheep, and we will know his voice. We will listen to his voice and obey him.

The process of learning to listen to God's voice in the spiritual realm is not unlike the process of learning to hear other voices in the physical realm. Why do we recognize voices of our parents, our spouse, our children, or our friends? We recognize their voices because we spend time with them and hear their voices often. Repetition provides familiarity. Therefore, the importance of spending time with the Lord to learn to hear his voice cannot be overemphasized. Intimacy with God takes time and regular interaction. There simply are no shortcuts. The ability to listen to God takes time to develop.

Morning by morning he wakens—wakens my ear to listen as those who are taught. The LORD GOD has opened my ear, and I was not rebellious, I did not turn backward. (Isaiah 50:4-5)

Listening also requires obedience. The hearing heart is one that is obedient. Consider Isaiah 50:4-5. When we purpose in our hearts to obey the instructions of the Lord, we will hear more clearly. Disobedience and rebellion to the ways of the Lord will hinder our ability to receive from God.

There are numerous hindrances to hearing God. Some of them include sin of any kind, concern and worry, preoccupation with self and responsibilities, and busyness and extra activities. Lack of teaching about listening to God may also hinder you. If it is still a revolutionary idea that the God of the universe wants to speak to you personally, accepting that truth may be a first step to receiving from the Lord. If you are sincerely struggling to hear from God, evaluate your life. Consider whether there are hindrances present that are blocking your relationship with the Lord. If God reveals unnecessary extra activities or busyness, for example, make a decision to deal with this hindrance. Humbly give the Lord permission to sift your schedule. Ask God to realign your priorities to give you sufficient time to wait on the Lord and listen.

Some other basic steps to hearing God include finding a quiet place and declaring your desire to hear from him. If your mind wanders as you are attempting to be quiet and listen, consider writing down your thoughts. The simple act of writing down your thoughts helps to sift what you are hearing. If it truly is a wandering thought like "we need chicken for dinner tonight," writing it down will help you to get back to the focus of hearing from the Lord during prayer. But don't be too quick to dismiss every thought as unnecessary. Quite simply, sometimes those unexpected thoughts are God saying, "This needs prayer."

If you are still unsure about what you hear, seek confirmation. Confirmation can come from the scriptures and from the counsel of others. In addition, learning to trust your own inner peace is important. Colossians 3:15 says, "And let the peace of Christ rule in your hearts." The peace of God is often the deciding factor for discerning guidance you hear from the Lord. Let peace *rule* like a referee. If God's peace that passes understanding is present, you are *safe* to move forward. If not, continue to wait on the Lord.

For many the dilemma in listening is how to know if it's really God. Here are some guidelines to compare the work of Christ with the work of Satan:

Christ convicts—Satan condemns.
Christ clarifies—Satan confuses.
Christ confirms—Satan contradicts.
Christ chooses—Satan captures.
Christ compels—Satan constricts.

This final guideline may be the most important of all. God will never contradict his Holy Word. Never. So if you hear something that is a contradiction to the scriptures, reject it. Steeping yourself in the Word of God is possibly the best way to grow in discernment. You'll be better able to hear those things that come from the Lord and more easily reject those things that are not in accord with God's revealed Word.

Although I have grown considerably in my listening ability, it is still probably the weakest area of my prayer life. I pray Isaiah 50:4-5 often, asking God for trained ears, ones that are being taught by the Lord. I'm learning to overcome my fear of silence and how to wait in God's presence for him to speak during prayer.

I understand better than ever that the condition of my heart really does affect my ability to hear from God. When I am rebellious, I will struggle to hear from God. I remember an incident many years ago that taught me a valuable lesson about listening. I was directing a vacation Bible school and needed an assistant. I was a person of prayer at this time and knew to ask the Lord in prayer before selecting an assistant. I prayed fervently for three days and heard absolutely nothing. Then, I did what many of us do; I did something in the flesh. I asked my friend to help me. My friend prayed about the opportunity and called me later that day to say that she did not feel led to be my assistant. However, she suggested the name of someone else. When I heard that name, my first reaction was, Oh no! I didn't want to hear that. Eventually, I asked this person to work with me, and we had a great experience working together. God softened my heart and changed the way I saw this person. Praise the Lord!

I learned a valuable lesson from that experience. Now, if I am asking the Lord a question and hear absolutely nothing after a season of prayer, I pray something like this, "OK, Lord, what am

I unwilling to hear this time." Absolute silence from the Lord has become a warning to me to examine my heart.

Another important lesson I've learned about listening is that guidance from the Lord is often like lampposts on the street. Just as one lamppost illuminates only part of the road and we need many lampposts to see the road ahead clearly, guidance from the Lord often comes in pieces or stages. We may just see enough light to make the next step. But if we take that step, God will continue to give light for succeeding steps. Every step of obedience increases our ability to hear from the Lord.

It truly was a revolutionary idea that God wanted to speak to me personally. Perhaps because of some of the baggage I brought into the Christian life, I struggled to believe that God wanted to talk to me about every aspect of my life. My experience of the baptism of the Holy Spirit was a decisive turning point. I had never heard God's voice before that life-changing experience. But after praying to receive the baptism of the Holy Spirit, I grew significantly in my ability to listen. The very next day, I heard the Lord's voice for the first time. I remember it like it was yesterday. The voice was so clear and audible that I actually turned around believing that someone was standing right next to me in the supermarket. And even though I've never again heard an audible voice like that experience, I've grown to hear God speak to me in many ways.

God speaks to me often through other people. In fact, I am so committed to unity in my marriage, that when Harry and I are seeking the Lord for guidance together I will often pray, "Lord, tell Harry." However, I realize that everything about listening is spiritually discerned. So I still must discern, *Oh yes, that is God speaking through Harry*. But I have come to embrace the ways God speaks through other people.

Unfortunately, before my baptism of the Holy Spirit I believe I was much more familiar with the voice of the enemy than the voice of God. Christ convicts and Satan condemns is true, but I was much more familiar with the voice of condemnation. Christ does convict us. Convict means "to prove guilty." When we sin, we will hear Christ's words of conviction. He convicts us in love. Christ's desire is to turn us back to the way that brings life. The conviction of the Lord will always be spoken with hope. That is a huge difference between conviction and condemnation. Condemnation attacks us at the core of our being and always passes judgment. Satan's condemnation will cause us to feel worthless and hopeless. God always offers hope. Satan never does.

Questions for Personal Reflection

1. God speaks in a variety of ways. Which ones are most familiar to you? Which ones are unfamiliar or more difficult for you?

2. What is the last thing God told you to do? Did you do it?

3. Reflect on the difference between the voice of the Lord and the voice of the enemy. Are you familiar with the voice of confusion or the voice of condemnation? Ask God for healing and a renewed sense of hearing his voice.

Activities for Small Groups

1. Learn to be better listeners by doing the following activity. Get in pairs. Decide who will speak first. Share something the Lord has done recently in your life. Spend about two minutes sharing. The partner who is designated to listen first should make no sound whatsoever, just listen. Often the reason we are not good listeners is because we are giving our attention to formulating our response. This activity removes that obstacle. Next, reverse roles and take turns listening.

Reflect on your experience. Was it difficult for you not to respond? Were you able to focus on giving your full attention to listening to your partner?

2. Focus on listening for God's guidance by doing the following activity. Get into pairs. Decide who will receive prayer first. The person designated to receive prayer does not share a prayer request with the partner. Instead he or she simply sits quietly in an attitude of receiving prayer. The partner designated to pray first silently asks God how to pray for the other person. You may receive a scripture, a thought, a vision, or some other direction from the Lord. Whatever you hear, pray silently for your partner. Next, reverse roles, so that the partner who prayed now becomes the recipient of prayer. Reflect on your experience. As you are comfortable, share with your partner how you prayed for him or her.

3. Pray Ephesians 1:16-19 over your partner. Ask God for the spirit of wisdom and revelation as you come to know him in listening prayer.

CHAPTER EIGHT

Praying the Scriptures

Praying the scriptures helps us to solve the dilemma, "I want to pray, but I just don't know what to say." When praying the Word of God for a particular need, we are never at a loss for how to pray. God's Word is full of promises and praying those promises gives voice to the cries of our heart in prayer.

Praying the scriptures is an important tool because it teaches us to *pray the promise* rather than to *pray the problem*. Sometimes we can get so caught up in telling God all about the problem during prayer that we forget God already knows every detail. Pouring our heart out to God when we are hurting is certainly a valuable part of prayer; however, if we stop there, we may never really see the victory in prayer. Instead, we can focus on the promises of God that are the answer to our needs.

What does the Bible say about praying the scriptures? Consider Isaiah 55:11. God's Word is the truth and it's powerful. By praying the scriptures, we can know that God's Word goes forth to accomplish his holy purposes. It will not return empty. We place our trust in God's faithfulness to honor his Holy Word.

. . . so shall my word be that goes out from my mouth; it shall not return to me empty, but it shall accomplish that which I purpose, and succeed in the thing for which I sent it. (Isaiah 55:11)

When we pray the scriptures, we are also following Jesus' example from Matthew 4:4. When faced with Satan's temptations in the wilderness, Jesus defeated the adversary with the Word. For each temptation he proclaimed, "It is written." Then Jesus spoke a specific scripture passage that countered Satan's attack.

And this is the boldness we have in him, that if we ask anything according to his will, he hears us. And if we know that he hears us in whatever we ask, we know that we have obtained the requests made of him. (1 John 5:14-15)

Why pray the scriptures? To follow Jesus' example is a great reason to start. But there are several other powerful reasons to learn to pray the scriptures. God's Word is his will, so we can know God's will from his Word. Do you want to pray according to God's will and see answers to prayer? Consider 1 John 5:14-15. Praying the scriptures gives us the confidence that God hears our prayers and will answer according to his will.

Praying the scriptures also allows us to focus on God's character and his desire to meet our needs. Rather than focusing on our needs when our hearts are burdened in prayer, we can focus on who God is, his love for us, and his provision for our needs.

How do we begin to incorporate this tool into our prayer lives? A great place to start is to use the scriptural prayers in the Bible and personalize them using your own name or the name of someone for whom you desire to intercede. Romans 15:13, Ephesians 1:15-19, Ephesians 3:14-21, Philippians 1:9-11 and Colossians 1:9-14 are all examples of prayers in the Bible. Here's Philippians 1:9-11 prayed for Margie:

> And this is my prayer, that [Margie's] love may overflow more and more with knowledge and full insight to help [Margie] to determine what is best, so that in the day of Christ [Margie] may be pure and blameless, having produced the harvest of righteousness that comes through Jesus Christ for the glory and praises of God.

Do you know someone who needs to experience God's love overflowing in his or her life today? Are you in need of wisdom "to determine what is best?" Pray this scripture today.

Ephesians 6:11-18 admonishes us to put on the whole armor of God. When we pray this important scripture, we can know the Lord's protection. The armor of God is not a mystical theory or theology. Think of it this way. Who is our peace? Who is our righteousness? Who is our truth? Jesus! So what are we putting on? We are clothing ourselves with Jesus and trusting that Christ will protect us from the deception of the enemy. Study the scriptures explaining the armor of God, and then determine to use each piece of the armor daily. Don't forget the "sword of the Spirit, which is the word of God." While many of the pieces of armor are defensive, the sword is clearly an offensive weapon. Learning to pray the Word pierces the enemy's schemes.

I love to pray the scriptures. I've come to believe that this is one of the most valuable tools in my spiritual toolbox. I've begun to use the Bible as my prayer book. When I am in prayer, I love to have an open Bible with me. I search God's word for his promises and personalize them for my needs or the needs of others. There are many helps available that I've used to focus my prayers on the promises of God. A good concordance will help you find appropriate topics. Several resources are listed in the bibliography that will help you know the promises of God for your life. However, the most important step I took was just crying out to God to orient my prayers on the scriptures. Allow the Holy Spirit to teach you to pray God's Word. "The one who calls you is faithful, and he will do this" (1 Thessalonians 5:24).

How do I know the will of God when I pray? It is contained in the Word. One special promise to me is 2 Peter 3:9: "The Lord is not slow about his promise, as some think of slowness, but is patient with you, not wanting any to perish, but all to come to repentance." Salvation of the lost is always God's will. Nobody I intercede for is outside of this promise. I can pray with absolute confidence that it is God's will that all come to know him. When the answer seems to tarry, I can focus on the character of God and remember that the Lord is never too slow to fulfill his promise. When I need perseverance, and I often do when praying for salvation for loved ones, I stand on the truth of God's Word.

I find I stand in need of praying the scriptures for myself often. I keep a whole list of scriptures in my journal that focus on "who I am in Christ." When the enemy assails my mind with harassing thoughts, I go to the scriptures in prayer. Some of my favorite promises are Philippians 4:13, Romans 8:37, and 1 Peter 2:9. Develop your own list and pray them like medicine for the healing for your mind.

Do your best to present yourself to God as one approved by him, a worker who has no need to be ashamed, rightly explaining the word of truth. (2 Timothy 2:15)

I am passionate about praying for the renewal of the church by the power of the Holy Spirit. However, I've learned that in the process of praying for the church I can sometimes focus on the problems I see and become discouraged. My prayers can take a downward spiral if they focus solely on the need. Therefore, I make praying the scriptures an important part of my prayers for the renewal of the church. For example, I love to pray 2 Timothy 2:15 for pastors. I do not have to become judgmental or critical; I simply pray the promises of God with confidence. The workbook *Pathways to a Praying Church*, available through Aldersgate Renewal Ministries, contains many helpful scriptural prayer guides for praying for pastors and spiritual leaders as well as the renewal of the church by the power of the Holy Spirit.

During my times of deepest burden in prayer, I turn to God's Word. For example, when my eldest son was involved in drugs as a teenager, I knew I needed to do more than just tell God about the problem. I spent much time seeking God, listening for his voice, and asking God for his promises for my children. I was reading the Good News Bible (TEV) at the time, so that translation of Jeremiah 31:16-17 was very special to me: "Stop your crying and wipe away your tears. All that you have done for your children will not go unrewarded; they will return from the enemy's land. There is hope for your future; your children will come back home. I, the Lord, have spoken." This scripture became the focal point of my prayers. I didn't know how or when God's promise would be fulfilled, but I became confident that God would answer my prayers. I experienced the fulfillment of that promise several years later. If you have prodigal children who are running from the Lord, let Jeremiah 31 bring you comfort and assurance. It is God's Word; it's the truth.

Questions for Personal Reflection

1. Consider your present prayer life. How likely are you to pray the scriptures when faced with a need?

2. Have you ever experienced a time when someone asked you to pray for his or her need and you did not know how to pray? Did you turn to scripture?

3. Using a concordance, search the scriptures for promises related to these needs:

    *   Grief, loss of a loved one
    *   Wisdom, guidance from the Lord
    *   Discouragement, lack of faith
    *   Peace in the midst of the storms of life

Activities for Small Groups

1. Choose one of the prayers from scripture referenced in this chapter and pray it for a partner.

    Romans 15:13
    Ephesians 1:15-19
    Ephesians 3:14-21
    Philippians 1:9-11
    Colossians 1:9-14

2. Read Psalm 91:9-14 and pray this prayer of protection. Note the conditions stated in verses 9 and 14.

CHAPTER NINE

Praying in the Name of Jesus

What is your name? Do you know the significance of your name? Were you named after another family member? Do you have a nickname? A name is simply a title by which a person or thing is known or designated. Names can also include titles that speak of a person's reputation or educational background. Knowing someone's family name can give clues to their family history.

"She will bear a son, and you are to name him Jesus, for he will save his people from their sins." (Matthew 1:21)

Unlike in our society today, names were considered very important in biblical times. Names were chosen to define a person's character or mission in life. They were to represent the child's essence or total character. Consider Matthew 1:21. The

Lord appeared to Joseph in a dream and directed him to name the baby Mary was carrying Jesus. It is significant that Jesus' name was designated on the basis of God's plan for his life before he was born. Names are important to God. God even changed some people's names in scripture following a dramatic, life-changing encounter. God changed Abram's name to Abraham in Genesis 17 and Jacob became Israel in Genesis 32.

Learning to pray in Jesus' name is an important tool in our prayer life. Consider Colossians 3:16-17. This scripture challenges us to do everything in the name of the Lord Jesus. Certainly, that includes prayer. When we pray in Jesus' name we are praying according to his character and his reputation. In addition, our prayers will always be offered in an attitude of gratitude "giving thanks to God the Father."

Let the word of Christ dwell in you richly; teach and admonish one another in all wisdom; and with gratitude in your hearts sing psalms, hymns and spiritual songs to God. And whatever you do, in word or deed, do everything in the name of the Lord Jesus, giving thanks to God the Father through him. (Colossians 3:16-17)

Why do we pray in Jesus' name? Jesus commanded us to pray in his name. Here's a challenging promise from John 14:13-14: "I will do whatever you ask in my name, so that the Father may be glorified in the Son. If in my name you ask me for anything, I will do it." When we pray in obedience to the Lord's command, the Lord promises to answer requests made in is name that will glorify him. Does that "If" catch your attention? It should. Learning what it means, and perhaps what it does not mean, to pray in Jesus' name is very important. Jesus' promise, "I will do it," is reserved for those prayers offered according to his will.

"I will do whatever you ask in my name, so that the Father may be glorified in the Son. If in my name you ask me for anything, I will do it." (John 14:13-14)

Another reason to pray in Jesus' name is because of the authority and power of the name. Philippians 2:9-11 reminds us that God gave Jesus his name. God exalted Jesus and gives him power and authority. One day every knee will bow before the Lord and every tongue will confess Jesus as Lord. This scripture has not yet been fulfilled; it awaits the Judgment. At the Judgment every tongue *will* confess that Jesus Christ is Lord. For some this will be a forced confession that does not reflect submission to the Lord. From that perspective, it is far better to choose now to bow the knee to Christ and to live under the power and authority in his name than to wait for the day when some will make that forced confession. There are wonderful benefits in prayer for the believer who knows the authority and power in the name of Jesus.

Jesus has been given all authority, "in heaven and on earth," according to Matthew 28:18-20. When we come under the Lord's authority, he willingly shares his authority with each of us in prayer. However, we have authority only if we are under authority. That "if" cannot be overlooked. Praying in the name of Jesus requires a surrendered will. Are you under the authority of Christ?

Knowing the power of Jesus' name is an important key to seeing signs and wonders, deliverance ministry, and spiritual, physical, and emotional healing in our lives and in our churches.

Consider James 5:14-15. When praying for the sick and anointing them with oil in the name of the Lord, we are following the direction of scripture. Clearly, our ministry must always be "in the name of the Lord." Jesus prayed and ministered in the power of the Holy Spirit and so must we. Under the direction of the Holy Spirit we can pray, "Be healed in Jesus' name."

Are any among you sick? They should call for the elders of the church and have them pray over them, anointing them with oil in the name of the Lord. The prayer of faith will save the sick, and the Lord will raise them up; and anyone who has committed sins will be forgiven. (James 5:14-15)

Praying in Jesus' name requires knowledge of God's Word. Knowing the promises of God help us know to what prayers Jesus would "sign his name." We see this truth in the secular world. Have you seen political advertisements that have this claim? "I'm (insert name of politician) and I approved this ad." These advertisements are claiming that the candidate gave his authorization and approval to use his name. The claims in the political advertisement are therefore his. In a similar way, God makes promises in the Word that he then authorizes believers to claim in prayer. Praying in Jesus' name begins with knowing the promises of the scriptures.

In Bible times, a king's ring was a symbol of his authority. Important documents, for example, were sealed with wax and imprinted with the king's signet ring. Persons recognized the authority and power of the king when they saw that symbol. The king also gave the ring to one of his ambassadors in a foreign country to do business on his behalf. The ambassador acted with the power and authority of the king. Consider 2 Corinthians 5:20. We are ambassadors of Christ! We have the name, the power, and the authority of Christ to empower our prayers. We are acting on his behalf.

So we are ambassadors for Christ, since God is making his appeal through us; we entreat you on behalf of Christ, be reconciled to God. (2 Corinthians 5:20)

To repeat, praying in the name of Jesus requires a surrendered will and knowledge of God's Word. It also requires an understanding of what praying in the name of Jesus is *not*. We can never use Jesus' name as a postscript to a selfish prayer. Sometimes we end our prayer with the words, "In the name of Jesus, Amen." An otherwise selfish prayer does not have more validity because we tack on the name of Jesus. In addition, we don't use Jesus' name as a "magician's wand" waving it about in hopes that God will answer prayers that are not in accordance with his will. As we pray in Jesus' name, we must be constantly submitting our will to the Lord and asking the Holy Spirit to direct our prayers.

Have I been caught in the trap of praying selfish prayers and tacking on the name of Jesus as a postscript? Yes, I have. What was the result? Mostly disappointment and sometimes confusion. When I am open to the voice of the Lord, I will hear him bring correction. Matthew 22:29 has been God's Word to me on several occasions: "Jesus answered them, 'You are wrong because you know neither the scriptures nor the power of God.'" God consistently sifts my prayers so that they agree with the Word. The cry of my heart is that the Lord's desires and purposes would be mine.

At renewal events in local churches and during conferences, I have the privilege of praying for individuals. Just as Jesus prayed and ministered in the power of the Holy Spirit, I am learning to do likewise. My desire is to be obedient to the Lord and minister in his name. So I pray in the name of Jesus and trust that God will honor his Word. The results are mixed. Sometimes God heals instantly, sometimes he heals over time. Sometimes the Lord's healing comes in eternity. Often there is evidence of emotional healing and freedom from bondages to the past. Also, spiritual healing and empowerment of the Holy Spirit are often experienced as I pray in Jesus' name. God's faithfulness is evident as I am seeing signs and wonders, deliverance ministry, and healing of body, soul, and spirit. Such faithfulness is a reminder that God does the healing, and we have the privilege of being his ambassadors. Praise the Lord!

Questions for Personal Reflection

1. Consider the statement, "We have authority only if we are under authority." Are there areas of your life that are not under the authority of Christ? Are your prayers empowered with the authority and power of Jesus' name?

2. Does "the word of Christ dwell in you richly" as we are instructed in Colossians 3:16-17? What changes do you need to make?

3. Meditate on Mark 16:17-18:

   > And these signs will accompany those who believe: by using my name they will cast out demons; they will speak in new tongues; they will pick up snakes in their own hands, and if they drink any deadly thing, it will not hurt them; they will lay hands on the sick, and they will recover.

   How is the authority and power of Jesus' name portrayed in this scripture?

4. In what area of your life do you need to pray, "In the name of Jesus" today? Do you have a spiritual or emotional need, for example, that you can take to the Lord in prayer?

Activities for Small Groups

1. Share with your prayer partners times when you have prayed, "In the name of Jesus."

2. Pray boldly, "In the name of Jesus," using these scriptures as a basis for your prayers:

   - For Wisdom—Pray that the word of Christ would dwell in you richly in all wisdom (Colossians 3:16-17).
   - For the Power of the Holy Spirit—Ask God to fill you with the power of the Holy Spirit to enable you to minister in the Spirit (Romans 8:15-17, 26).
   - For Healing—Pray for healing of the sick (James 5:14-15).

CHAPTER TEN

Intercession: Praying for Others

Intercession is defined as praying for others. It is coming to God on behalf of another in much the same way a mediator pleads our case before one in authority. We can petition God for our own needs, but we cannot intercede for ourselves. Intercession is always other-centered.

Intercession is the prayer ministry of all believers. I believe intercession is also one of the gifts of the Holy Spirit. Those with this gift of the Spirit can carry a larger burden in prayer and intercession. Intercessors are sometimes easily identified. They find great joy in praying for others. However, the Lord never intended intercession to be the sole responsibility of the intercessors. Every believer must be equipped and empowered to fulfill that role. Have you discovered your part in the ministry of intercession?

What does the Bible say about intercession? Consider Isaiah 59:15b-16a and Ezekiel 22:30. These scriptures indicate that a lack of intercession displeases God and withholds his mercy.

> *The* Lord *saw it, and it displeased him that there was no justice. He saw that there was no one, and was appalled that there was no one to intervene.* (Isaiah 59:15b-16a)

Isaiah 59 outlines grievous sins of the Israelite people. The chapter includes doing works of iniquity and deeds of violence, transgressing and denying the Lord, talking oppression and revolt, conceiving lying words and uttering them from the heart. Still, the Lord was appalled that there was no one to intervene.

> *And I sought for anyone among them who would repair the wall and stand in the breach before me on behalf of the land, so that I would not destroy it; but I found no one.* (Ezekiel 22:30)

Ezekiel 22 is a summary of Jerusalem's sins. They include these condemning words: "You have despised my holy things, and profaned my sabbaths" (verse 8), "commit lewdness" (verse 9), "take bribes to shed blood" and "make gain . . . by extortion" (verse 12). Amazingly, God was still looking for someone to intercede in prayer—someone who would come before him on behalf of the sinful people and cry out for mercy.

Where was someone who would, "stand in the breach"? City walls were important in Bible times. Warriors in armor were called out to stand in the gap when a break or crumbling part of the wall occurred. Likewise, *standing in the gap* is the role of the intercessor in prayer. In Ezekiel 22, God's justice demanded punishment for the sins of the people, and the people of Israel deserved destruction; but his heart desired mercy. Who would pray and intercede, "so that I would not destroy it"? Regrettably, God found no one. Verse 31 gives the predictable result:

"Therefore I have poured out my indignation upon them; I have consumed them with the fire of my wrath; I have returned their conduct upon their heads, says the LORD GOD."

These scriptures cause us to reflect on the role of the intercessor. Have you given up on people or circumstances? Have you judged situations too sinful or grievous for intercession? God is still looking for those who will intervene in prayer. Will you answer God's call to intercession?

Hebrews 7:24-25 tells us about Jesus' role in intercession. Where is Jesus today? Jesus, in his glorified body, is seated beside God the Father in heaven. His role as our High Priest is to make intercession for the saints. Jesus is praying for you and me! Let the truth of that scripture grip your heart and mind. There is joy, protection, and security in that knowledge.

And all of us, with unveiled faces, seeing the glory of the Lord as though reflected in a mirror, are being transformed into the same image from one degree of glory to another; for this comes from the Lord, the Spirit.
(2 Corinthians 3:18)

Now consider 2 Corinthians 3:18. God's Holy Spirit lives within us and is constantly changing us to reflect his glory. We are being transformed from glory unto glory, ever becoming more like Christ. That is good news! This truth will influence our prayer life and how we intercede for others. As we are transformed and equipped by the Holy Spirit, we *will* take up our role in intercession. Glory to God!

The Holy Spirit also has a role in intercession. Consider Romans 8:26-27. The Spirit, "helps us in our weakness," when we do not know how to pray. Sometimes we will intercede with sighs and groans, wordless prayers that are understood by the

Father. Sometimes the Spirit will inspire our words and give us wisdom to pray according to his will. We need to learn to embrace the role of the Holy Spirit in enabling us to pray and intercede for others.

Likewise the Spirit helps us in our weakness; for we do not know how to pray as we ought, but that very Spirit intercedes with sighs too deep for words. And God, who searches the heart, knows what is the mind of the Spirit, because the Spirit intercedes for the saints according to the will of God. (Romans 8:26-27)

The Old Testament has numerous examples of intercession. Abraham interceded for Sodom (Genesis 18:20-33 and Genesis 19:29); Moses interceded for the Hebrew people (Exodus 32:11-14); Moses and Aaron interceded for the assembly (Numbers 16:1-48). Study these scriptures to understand more fully the role of the intercessor. Each one is an example of fervent prayers on behalf of the sins of the people and crying out for God's mercy.

The New Testament also has powerful examples of intercession. Jesus prays for Simon Peter (Luke 22:31-32); Jesus prays for himself, his disciples, and for all believers (John 17); Paul prays for the saints (Romans 1:8-10, Ephesians 1:15-21, Philippians 1:3-11, and Colossians 1:3-9); we are to pray for one another (James 5:13-20). Scriptures indicate that intercession is vitally important. What part does intercession for others play in your prayer life?

One of my primary gifts from the Holy Spirit is intercession. Therefore, God often gives me opportunity to exercise this gift in the body of Christ. I love to pray for others and find great fulfillment in spending time in intercession. However, the intercessor's passion for prayer or practice of extended time in solitary prayer can cause misunderstanding. As with any gift of the Spirit, we need to be aware of comparison and judgmentalism.

Comparing my prayer life to others without this gift is not helpful. When others don't seem to *pray enough*, I can be too quick to point out their problem or judge them as weak. With God's correction, I'm learning to appreciate and embrace the prayers of all people. I've discovered that the reverse can also be true. People without the gift of intercession may compare their prayer life to someone with this gift and become discouraged. Comparison can lead to damaged feelings of *never measuring up* or simply leaving intercession to the *real prayer warriors*. Either form of comparison can be harmful if it prevents prayer for others. God intends all believers to have a role in intercession.

I thought I understood the instruction of Ezekiel 22:30 for a long time before God brought revelation and a change of heart. "Stand in the breach" is not the whole instruction. Instead, this scripture instructs us to "Stand in the breach before me on behalf of the land." Do you discern a difference? God spoke clearly to me about the absolute necessity of a pure heart, submission to the Lord, and intimacy with him as requirements of an intercessor. God was calling me to a new level of accountability. I cannot go before God on behalf of others with sin in my life. I must come to the point of being able to stand before God without any walls of deception or impure motives. All this is by God's grace and according to his mercy. Personal preparation for the ministry of intercession has become a necessity for me.

When I consider Ezekiel 22 and the grievous sins of the people, I know that I too have been guilty of a lack of intercession. There have been times I've *written people off*, given up on them as hopeless, and grieved the heart of God. I now understand that when the Lord gives a burden in prayer I must continue to pray and persevere, waiting on God's intervention. Without the Holy Spirit's empowerment, I will fail miserably.

As much as I love to intercede for the personal needs of others, my passion is to pray for the renewal of the church by the power of the Holy Spirit. Much of my time of intercession involves praying for pastors and spiritual leaders to be full of the Holy Spirit and leading their people as faithful shepherd leaders. In addition, I love to pray for churches to become houses of prayer where corporate prayer and intercession in groups is a priority. I make an intentional effort to network with other intercessors who share my burden for intercession for the church.

God has shown me that the gifting and calling of people to intercession varies greatly. God the Father, in his infinite wisdom, gives prayer burdens as he knows best. Whether our burden is large or small, God simply asks us to be obedient. When God called me to my role as Director of Prayer Ministries with Aldersgate Renewal Ministries (ARM), he gave me a vision of an intercessors prayer network that would undergird the ministry of ARM in prayer and intercede for the renewal of the church. I saw the Lord standing beside a large farm wagon. In the wagon were stones of various sizes and shapes. The stones symbolized prayer burdens that God wanted people to carry. Jesus stood beside the farm wagon handing out stones to people as they filed past. I was particularly drawn to watch Jesus' face. His eyes showed the same love and affirmation for each person that received their stone—whether it was large or small. Which stone is yours to carry? Will you be obedient to the Lord?

Questions for Personal Reflection

1. Do you have the gift of intercession? Consider taking a spiritual gift inventory. One excellent resource is *Rediscovering*

Our Spiritual Gifts by Charles Bryant. Reflect on these characteristics of persons with the gift of intercession:

- I have a special sense of knowing when others need my prayers.
- When I hear requests for prayer, I eagerly and immediately begin to pray.
- Praying is my most enjoyable spiritual activity.
- I am moved to pray for others—even though I may not know them—and for conditions about which I know very little.
- I feel urges to pray for others to be empowered for effective ministries. (Bryant, 1991, 163–176)

2. Do you know someone who is an intercessor? Consider encouraging that person's gift from the Holy Spirit.

3. What role does intercessory prayer play in your current prayer life?

4. Reflect on Jesus' prayer in John 17. Verse 10 (NIV) says, "Glory has come to me through them." Does your prayer life bring God glory?

5. In John 17, Jesus prayed for unity in the body of Christ (verse 11), for our protection from the evil one (verse 15), and for our purity and holiness in the truth (verse 17). How are Jesus' prayers reflected in your prayers and intercession?

Activities for Small Groups

1. Share a need briefly with a partner. Intercede for each other for the specific need.

2. Pray together for someone else you know who has a need.

3. As a group, intercede for our nation, the church, or a world situation that God places on your heart. Ask God to direct your prayers.

CHAPTER ELEVEN

Praying the Names of God

When you address God in prayer, what name do you use most often? Jesus taught us to pray, "Our Father" and that is a very appropriate way to address God. As we study scripture, however, we see that God has revealed himself with a variety of other names that enhance our knowledge of who God is. Praying the revealed names of God from scripture can enrich our prayer life and give us a powerful vocabulary of praise.

You believe that God is one; you do well. Even the demons believe—and shudder. (James 2:19)

Praying the names of God also means calling on the power and authority of God as revealed in his names. God's name has power and authority. Even the demons know God's name and tremble. As believers, we are not to be fearful of God, but rather to bow before him in humility and reverent submission to his name. We call upon God in prayer, recognizing his personality as revealed in his names. We add power to our prayers when we learn to praise God for who he is, and then intercede according to the revealed names of God. We do not have to beg God to be who God says he is. We just call upon God, for example, with the power and authority of "El Shaddai, God Almighty" (Genesis 17:1).

In addition to calling on the power and authority of God, God's name reveals his nature. God's name helps us to understand his power and authority, his eternal existence. To God alone belongs honor and worship. For example, the name Jehovah means, "I am, the eternal living one" (Exodus 3:14).

> The Jews scrupulously avoided every mention of this name of God, substituting in its stead one or other of the words with whose proper vowel-points it may happen to be written. This custom, which had its origin in reverence, was founded upon an erroneous rendering of Leviticus 24:16, from which it was inferred that the mere utterance of the name constituted a capital offense. According to Jewish tradition, it was pronounced but once a year, by the high priest on the day of atonement when he entered the holy of holies. (*Smith's Bible Dictionary*)

The Jews became morbidly afraid of blasphemy. Their fear was great because the cost was extreme. Therefore, faithful Jews did not dare to even speak the name of God. This erroneous rendering of scripture is an example of the Pharisees' zealous interpretation of law. Interestingly, Jesus brought change to this understanding of addressing God. In the New Testament, Jesus taught his disciples to call God Father. Rather than shun calling on God by name, Jesus instructed the disciples to address God as Father using the familiar term of *Abba*, which could be translated as Papa or Daddy.

And those who know your name put their trust in you, for you, O LORD have not forsaken those who seek you. (Psalm 9:10)

Knowing God's name builds trust in God. Consider Psalm 9:10 and Isaiah 50:10. Studying the revealed names of God builds our faith and total reliance on the Lord. Do you need God's provision today? Call upon God as *Jehovah-Jireh*, which means "The Lord will provide" (Genesis 22:14). Are you or your loved ones in need of the healing touch of God today? Call upon the Lord in prayer as *Jehovah-Rophe*, which means "the Lord our healer" (Exodus 15:26). Then put your trust in God alone and know that he has not forsaken you.

Who among you fears the LORD and obeys the voice of his servant, who walks in darkness and has no light, yet trusts in the name of the LORD and relies upon his God? (Isaiah 50:10)

Why pray the revealed names of God? The names of God also provide a powerful source for adoration. Expressing adoration can greatly enhance our ability to honor God for who he is and teach us to hallow his name. The Lord's Prayer, our model prayer, articulates such reverence: "Our Father in heaven, hallowed be your name" (Matthew 6:9). We need a rich vocabulary of praise.

How do you get started? Search the scriptures for a name of God that speaks to your prayer need. Praise God for his character revealed in that name. Then petition God to answer your prayer in the power of his name. Finally, trust God to answer your prayer. God is faithful to his name and promises. At the close of this chapter is a chart that contains some of the revealed names of God. This chart can be an aid as you begin your journey using this powerful tool for personal prayer.

When I stand in need of a deeper revelation of who God is,
I often pray the names of God. For example, when Abram was
ninety-nine years old, the Lord appeared to him as *El Shaddai*
and said, "I am God Almighty; walk before me, and be blameless"
(Genesis 17:1). When we know who God is, I believe it affects
our desire to live a holy life. The cry of my heart is often, "God
Almighty, help me to walk in holiness before you."

I have found *Jehovah-Rophe* to bring me great comfort when
I need healing. I acknowledge that God is *the Lord who heals*. My
healing is based on the character of God and his desire to heal.
Jehovah-Rophe literally means "to mend by stitches." I have often
seen God's healing come in stages as he mends my emotions, for
example, one stitch at a time. I take comfort in the fact that each
step of the healing is part of God's plan to bring me to wholeness. I'm learning to trust God's perfect timing and acknowledge
with praise each aspect of God's healing of my mind, my will,
and my emotions.

In Exodus 15, God tested the Israelites at the waters of
Marah. The waters were bitter and God instructed Moses to
throw a piece of wood into the water to make it sweet. He said,
"If you will listen carefully to the voice of the LORD your God,
and do what is right in his sight, and give heed to his commandments and keep all his statutes, I will not bring upon you any of
the diseases that I brought upon the Egyptians; for I am the
LORD who heals you" (Exodus 15:26). I understand this to be
one of many conditional promises in scripture. Our part is to listen carefully to the voice of the Lord and to obey the
commandments of the Lord. When I am calling on the Lord as
my *Jehovah-Rophe*, I'm learning to ask God to sift my heart and
my thoughts. If God reveals any areas of disobedience, I take that
correction seriously. Confession of sin and total reliance on God

to honor his name are becoming important aspects of my personal prayer life.

PRAYING THE NAMES OF GOD

Name	Meaning	Reference
Adonai	Lord, Master	Isaiah 6:1
Alpha and Omega	*Beginning and the end of all*	*Revelation 22:13*
Ancient of Days	Judge of the whole world	Daniel 7:9
Elohim	*Creator*	*Genesis 1:1*
El Elyon	The Most High God	Genesis 14:18
El Gmolah	*Lord God of Recompenses*	*Jeremiah 51:56*
El Olam	The Everlasting God	Genesis 21:33
El Ro'i	*Strong One Who Sees*	*Genesis 16:13*
Holy Spirit	Righteous, present with us	Titus 3:5
Jehovah-hoseem	*The Lord Our Maker*	*Psalm 95:6*
Jehovah-jireh	The Lord Will Provide	Genesis 22:14
Jehovah-M'kaddesh	*The Lord Who Sanctifies You*	*Leviticus 20:8*
Jehovah-nissi	The Lord My Banner	Exodus 17:15
Jehovah-rophe	*The Lord Our Healing*	*Exodus 15:26*
Jehovah-sabaoth	The Lord of Hosts	Psalm 59:5
Jehovah-shalom	*The Lord Is Peace*	*Judges 6:24*
Jehovah-shammah	The Lord Is There	Ezekiel 48:35
Jehovah-tsidkenu	*The Lord Our Righteousness*	*Jeremiah 23:6*
Qanna	Jealous	Exodus 34:14
Yahweh	*Lord (Jehovah)*	*Psalm 11:4*

And those who know your name put their trust in you, for you, O LORD, have not forsaken those who seek you. (Psalm 9:10)

Questions for Personal Reflection

1. Consider your prayer life. How likely are you to pray the revealed names of God when faced with a need?

2. Do you pray in the power and authority of God's name? What circumstances in your life need God's power and authority today?

3. The Lord's Prayer is our model prayer. Do you hallow God's name in prayer? Could praying God's revealed names enrich your vocabulary of praise?

Activities for Small Groups

1. Share briefly a prayer need with your small group. Intercede for one another using the revealed names of God from this lesson. Call upon the Lord in prayer, trusting him to honor his name.

2. Use the names of God as a source of adoration in prayer. Attempt to spend five minutes in prayer praising God without asking for anything.

CHAPTER TWELVE

Praying Hymns

In Old Testament times, the Psalms constituted the hymn treasury of the temple. The Psalter was recognized as the temple "hymnbook" and singing was recognized as a form of prayer. Today praying hymns can be a tool to enrich our personal prayer lives.

I will extol you, O LORD, for you have drawn me up, and did not let my foes rejoice over me. O LORD my God, I cried to you for help, and you have healed me. O LORD, you brought up my soul from Sheol, restored me to life from among those gone down to the Pit. Sing praises to the LORD, O you his faithful ones, and give thanks to his holy name. (Psalm 30:1-4)

A hymn is defined as a song or ode in praise of the Lord. An ode is a poem that was written to be sung. Although the tunes for the Psalms are no longer known, many of the Psalms were written to be sung in praise of God. One example is Psalm 30 that was, "a song at the dedication of the temple." David wrote this Psalm and addressed it to God, giving thanks to God for all he had done. It is a song of adoration and thanksgiving. Part of the Psalm is also petitioning prayer. "Hear, O LORD, and be gracious to me! O LORD, be my helper!" (Psalm 30:10). We would do well to echo David's prayer today, whether it is spoken or sung.

Introductory instructions to the Levite singers precede many of the Psalms. These instructions help us to understand that the Psalms were meant to be sung. Psalms 80–83 are good examples.

Now these are the singers, the heads of ancestral houses of the Levites, living in the chambers of the temple free from other service, for they were on duty day and night. (1 Chronicles 9:33)

David also commanded the chiefs of the Levites to appoint their kindred as the singers to play on musical instruments, on harps and lyres and cymbals, to raise loud sounds of joy. (1 Chronicles 15:16)

These are the men whom David put in charge of the service of song in the house of the LORD, after the ark came to rest there. They ministered with song before the tabernacle of the tent of meeting, until Solomon had built the house of the LORD in Jerusalem; and they performed their service in due order. (1 Chronicles 6:31-32)

During the time of David, he organized 4,000 musicians and 288 singers to minister to God in shifts that continued 24 hours a day. (See 1 Chronicles 6:31-32 and 15:16-22 for more details.) This was apparently their full-time occupation (1 Chronicles 9:33). Worship in David's day was continuous, skillful, creative, joyful, extravagant, and strategic. Praying the Psalms can help us replicate that style of worship and prayer.

Psalm 107 was probably sung at the first feast of the tabernacles chronicled in Ezra 3. When the Jews under Nehemiah were repairing the walls of Jerusalem, the workmen and guards—while engaged in their respective duties—probably sang Psalms 120–134. All these examples help us to see how the Psalms were used for prayer and worship by the Israelites.

Old Testament hymns outside the Psalter have also been preserved. Examples are the song of Moses (Exodus 15:1-19 and Deuteronomy 32:1-45), the song of Deborah and Barak (Judges 5), and the song of Hannah (I Samuel 2:1-10).

Exodus 15 is representative of a song outside the Psalter used as a tool for worship and prayer. Moses and the Israelites sang this song to the Lord following their deliverance from Pharaoh. The song tells the story of God's victory and exalts God as the one who, "In the greatness of your majesty you overthrew your adversaries" (Exodus 15:7).

"I will sing to the LORD, for he has triumphed gloriously; horse and rider he has thrown into the sea. The LORD is my strength and my might, and he has become my salvation; this is my God, and I will praise him, my father's God, and I will exalt him. The LORD is a warrior; the LORD is his name." (Exodus 15:1-3)

There are several other examples of hymns or songs from the Bible. For example, Jesus and his disciples sang a hymn (Matthew 26:30 and Mark 14:26); Mary's "Magnificat" (Luke 1:46-55); Paul and Silas prayed and sang hymns (Acts 16:25). It is believed that the hymn that Jesus and his disciples sang at the conclusion of the Last Supper was probably the Hallel, Psalm 113-118. From all these examples in scripture we can see that singing has long been recognized as a form of prayer and worship.

Let the word of Christ dwell in you richly; teach and admonish one another in all wisdom; and with gratitude in your hearts sing psalms, hymns, and spiritual songs to God. (Colossians 3:16)

Several times in the New Testament believers are admonished to sing and pray. Some examples are Ephesians 5:19, James 5:13, and Colossians 3:16. We are all instructed to sing to the Lord. Interestingly, there is no mention of musical ability or lack of it. Our songs are to come from a grateful heart and be expressions of thanksgiving and adoration to God.

Praying hymns has often enriched my prayer life. Although I am "musically challenged," I love to sing praises to the Lord and find the hymns a wonderful addition to my prayers. However, I also use the hymnal as a tool for prayer by reading and praying the words of the hymns.

On several occasions, I've used resources like *Song Stories* by Lucy Adams to research the history behind the hymn. Knowing the circumstances of the author's life helps me to identify with the song and pray the words to the Lord. A good example is "O For a Thousand Tongues" by Charles Wesley. Adams makes this comment about the song:

It was the day his life changed—Sunday, May 21, 1738. For Charles Wesley the assurance of his salvation in Jesus Christ went from his head to his heart on that memorable day. A year later he celebrated the experience with the writing of a hymn, sparked when, according to history, a fellow minister joyfully remarked to Wesley, "Had I a thousand tongues I would praise Jesus with them all." (Adams, 1998, 15)

I identify with Charles' jubilant praise and thanksgiving for a changed life and love to sing and pray this hymn.

You probably have personal favorite hymns too. Another favorite of mine is "It is Well with My Soul" by Horatio Spafford. I identify with his time of sorrow and the living faith God gave him in spite of his circumstances. His words, written in poem form, were penned at a time of deep tragedy. Horatio's beloved daughters were lost at sea. Here's what Adams says about this hymn story:

> In this father's time of grief he spoke to his Lord who had taught him to have this attitude: "When peace like a river, attendeth my way, When sorrows like sea billows roll, Whatever my lot, Thou has taught me to say, It is well, it is well with my soul." Mr. Spafford's strong faith, displayed in the verses of this beloved hymn, is a witness to the power of a loving God who can heal the brokenhearted. (Adams, 1998, 9)

Praying hymns is enhanced when we recognize the variety of topics they cover. There are hymns appropriate for praise, for strength in tribulation and grief, for repentance, for personal holiness and for guidance—just to name a few. Included in this chapter is a chart to help you begin to use praying hymns as a tool for personal prayer. However, don't be limited by these examples. Do your own research, and enjoy singing and praying the Psalms.

HYMNS TO PRAY

Praise
How Great Thou Art ♦
All Hail the Power of Jesus Name ♦
There's Something about That Name ♦

My Jesus, I Love Thee
Jesus, the Very Thought of Thee

Sanctifying and Perfecting Grace
Spirit of the Living God
Jesus Remember Me
Jesus Lover of My Soul
O Love That Will Not Let Me Go
Spirit of God, Descend upon My Heart

Strength in Tribulation and Grief
Stand by Me
Nearer My God to Thee
Through It All
Leave It There
What a Friend We Have in Jesus

Repentance, Rebirth and New Creation
Have Thine Own Way Lord
Something Beautiful
Lord, I Want to Be a Christian
Just As I Am, Without One Plea
I Surrender All

Personal Holiness
O Jesus, I Have Promised
I Need Thee Every Hour
Take My Life and Let It Be
I Am Thine, O Lord
Breathe on Me, Breath of God

Guidance

Lead Me, Lord
Precious Lord, Take My Hand ◊
Jesus, Savior, Pilot Me
Savior Like a Shepherd Lead Us
Guide Me, O Thou Great Jehovah

Questions for Personal Reflection

1. Consider your personal prayer life. How likely are you to sing a prayer to the Lord?

2. Have you ever spoken the words of a hymn for a personal prayer?

3. Do you have a favorite hymn? What about that hymn speaks to your heart?

4. Worship in David's day was continuous, skillful, creative, joyful, extravagant, and strategic. Do you see these attributes of corporate prayer and worship being restored in our day? Do you desire or expect God to do this in your local church?

Activities for Small Groups

1. Choose a hymn that meets a prayer need in the group. Pray the words of the hymn together. Model several ways to use these hymns.

    - Pray the first verse silently.
    - Ask a leader to pray the second verse aloud as others in the group meditate on the words.
    - Pray the third verse aloud together slowly.
    - Sing the next verse together.

2. As a group, do some research into the history of your favorite hymns.

CHAPTER THIRTEEN

A-C-T-S

Adoration, Confession, Thanksgiving and Supplication (A-C-T-S) are important aspects of prayer. Each has a place in the prayer life of believers. Having a balanced model or tool that engages us in conversation with God can enhance our personal prayer life. The A-C-T-S model helps us to find balance and completeness when we pray. Let's look at each aspect of the model. We begin with adoration in the same way that the Lord's Prayer begins with, "Our Father who art in heaven, hallowed be thy name."

Adoration is defined as worshipping or paying homage, as to a divinity. Adoration is attributing honor and praising God for who he is, not just thanking God for what he does. Meditate on that truth and consider your current prayer life. Do you spend time in adoration of God? Thanksgiving is an important aspect of prayer, but it is not adoration.

Adoration is seeking the face of God and not the hand of God. Seeking God's face means coming into his presence to be

honor him as the God of the uni-
ith asking God for anything, which
ns of adoration, we are never seek-
's righteous right hand is powerful,
we need; however, supplication
nes of praise and adoration in our

---

*Though the fig tree does not blossom, and no fruit is on the
vines; though the produce of the olive fails, and the fields
yield no food; though the flock is cut off from the fold, and
there is no herd in the stalls, yet I will rejoice in the LORD;
I will exult in the God of my salvation.* (Habakkuk 3:17-18)

Adoration is based on the character of God and never on our
circumstances. Consider Habakkuk 3:17-18. This scripture indi-
cates that exalting and adoring God is not based on what God
does or does not do. Even when crops fail (economic woes) and
flocks cease (provision is bleak), there is still reason to adore God.
Revelation 4:11 reminds us, "You are worthy, our Lord and God,
to receive glory and honor and power, for you created all things,
and by your will they existed and were created." The God of creation is still worthy of praise regardless of our circumstances.

Scripture outlines some benefits of adoration. Adoration
focuses our prayers on God rather than on our problems. We
look up to God rather than down at our current burdens.
Adoration causes us to remember who God is. When we gaze on
God in adoration, he blasts strongholds of self-centeredness and
selfishness. It is impossible to praise God and stay in self-pity. Try
praising and adoring God the next time you sink into self-pity.
Praise is powerful. Adoration completely changes our focus away
from ourselves and on to God.

When he had taken counsel with the people, he appointed those who were to sing to the Lord and praise him in holy splendor, as they went before the army, saying, "Give thanks to the Lord for his steadfast love endures forever." As they began to sing and praise, the Lord set an ambush against the Ammonites, Moab, and Mount Seir, who had come against Judah, so that they were routed. (2 Chronicles 20:21-22)

Through him, then, let us continually offer a sacrifice of praise to God, this is, the fruit of lips that confess his name. (Hebrews 13:15)

Praise is also powerful spiritual warfare. Consider 2 Chronicles 20:21-22. When the enemy surrounded Jehoshaphat, God gave him the spiritual weapon of praise and adoration to defeat those who came to destroy the people of Judah and Jerusalem. Those appointed to praise God went out in front of the army and the enemy was routed. This same principle is true today. God has given us the tool of adoration to defeat the enemy.

Adoration often involves offering a *sacrifice of praise*. Consider Hebrews 13:15. These challenging words help us to understand that praise is a choice. Sacrifices should cost us something. Choosing to praise God in the midst of difficult circumstances is often a sacrifice. It will cost us our own agenda and our own self-interest, but it is a choice that God will bless.

If we confess our sins, he who is faithful and just will forgive us our sins and cleanse us from all unrighteousness. (1 John 1:9)

Confession is the next aspect of the A-C-T-S model. Confession can be defined as agreeing with God about our sins. Being willing to call sin, *sin* and seeking God's forgiveness is an important part of our daily prayer life. Confession has a parallel in the Lord's Prayer as well. Jesus taught us to pray, "And forgive us our debts, as we forgive our debtors." Confession of sin that leads to repentance and a true change of heart is a powerful source of transformation. We can trust that God is faithful to his Word and will always forgive us and cleanse us when we come to him in confession.

It is helpful to stay current with God. If we daily seek God's forgiveness rather than tactics like denial, rationalization, or passing the blame, we will grow closer to God. If we attempt to hide our sin from God or let it accumulate, we'll soon experience a wall of separation between God and us. We can understand the consequences of sin and still be unwilling to deal with our sin. Perhaps that is because confession of sin is not our natural inclination. It takes God's grace and mercy at work in our lives to truly make confession a vital part of our prayer life.

Give thanks in all circumstances; for this is the will of God in Christ Jesus for you. (1 Thessalonians 5:18)

Do not worry about anything, but in everything by prayer and supplication with thanksgiving let your requests be made know to God. (Philippians 4:6)

After we bring to God our confessions of sin, thanksgiving for his forgiveness of our sins should follow naturally. Thanksgiving, the third aspect of prayer, means saying thank you to the Lord for what he has done. Numerous scriptures remind us of the importance of thanksgiving. However, many of us are like the ten lepers in Luke 17:11-19. Only one returned to say thank you.

Unfortunately, we also neglect to come back to the Lord and offer thanks for the wonderful things he does for us. Large and small, significant or seemingly insignificant, each prayer need brought to the Lord deserves a proper *thank you* when God provides. Thanksgiving should be a vital part of our daily prayer lives.

The benefits of thanksgiving in prayer are abundant. When we remember all God has done in the past, we face the future with greater confidence and peace. By looking back to say thank you, our trust in God's ability to answer our prayers in the present grows. Thanksgiving always magnifies the Lord. Therefore, God appears larger and our problems seem smaller. That's the perspective we need to have when the circumstances of life are difficult. In addition, a thankful heart overflows to our relationships with others. What we experience with God will help us to be thankful in our relationships with other people. Thankful people are a joy to be around. Their heart of gratitude builds lasting relationships and helps friendships endure.

After we have spent time in adoration, confession, and thanksgiving, A-C-T-S prepares us for supplication. Supplication is defined as a humble request or a petition in prayer. It is asking God in prayer. Many people start their prayers with supplication; this model places our petitions last. When we've adequately honored God for who he is, when we have confessed our sins and received God's forgiveness, when we have thanked him for his forgiveness and all the other wonderful things he provides, the focus of our prayer requests will often be quite different. The Lord's priorities will likely become our priorities. Our requests will become conformed to God's will. That transformation is significant and will lead to greater delight in prayer.

"I will do whatever you ask in my name, so that the Father may be glorified in the Son. If in my name, you ask me for anything, I will do it." (John 14:13-14)

Since, "Your Father knows what you need before you ask him," (Matthew 6:8) a frequent question is simply *why ask?* There are benefits to asking God specifically in prayer. First, when we ask for something according to God's will, the Father is glorified in our prayers (John 14:13-14). That should be our primary motivation—to glorify God. Second, asking God in prayer and then gratefully receiving the provision builds faith. We learn that God is faithful to his promises, and we are more likely to come to God in prayer in the future. In addition, answered prayer is a primary source of our thanksgiving. The cycle of prayer continues.

I love the A-C-T-S model because it brings balance to my prayer life. In the past I often came to God with only supplications and petitions. I now begin my prayers with adoration and praise. In the following concluding paragraphs, I will convey the affect of the A-C-T-S model on my prayer life.

When I begin prayer with adoration, I experience God's presence. This sets the tone for all that follows. Also, I'm learning to offer a "sacrifice of praise." Even when I come to God with tears in my eyes and pain in my heart, I can choose to praise and adore him. When I make the decision to adore God first, he brings healing, encouragement, strength, and joy in the midst of my circumstances.

As I move from adoration to confession during my prayer time, I identify with the prophet Isaiah in Isaiah 6:1-5: "In the year that King Uzziah died, I saw the Lord sitting on a throne, high and lofty; and the hem of his robe filled the temple." Seeing the Lord high and lifted up is true adoration. Notice Isaiah's response in verse 5: "And I said: 'Woe is me! I am lost, for I am a man of unclean lips.'" When we truly encounter God, often our first response is to recognize our own sinfulness. I've seen this scripture fulfilled numerous times both in my own personal times of prayer as well as in times of corporate prayer and worship. When I encounter God, I become aware of my own pride and stubbornness. Then confession and repentance will follow. I cry out to God like David did in Psalm 51:1: "Have mercy on me, O God, according to your steadfast love; according to your abundant mercy blot out my transgressions."

God is also teaching me the importance of confessing my sins to others. Confession of sin, in the setting of prayer with others, has brought me much healing and release of bondage from my past. First Peter 2:9 reminds us that we are, "a royal priesthood." To have a trusted brother or sister in Christ look me in the eye and say, "In the name of Jesus Christ you are forgiven" is truly powerful. That kind of accountability in prayer brings freedom and maturity, and I recommend it.

What is your response to the lavish and undeserved forgiveness and mercy of God? Thanksgiving should be! We need to keep a *short* list of sins in our daily relationship with God, but we need to have a *lengthy* list of thanksgiving in prayer. More and more, I'm seeing God build thanksgiving into my life. It is significant that God's Word (1 Thessalonians 5:18) says we should, "Give thanks in all circumstances; for this is the will of God . . . for you." Since it is God's will for me, I know that it is possible and that the Holy Spirit is God's provision to live out this command. I'm learning to live by God's Word.

Thanksgiving also prepares us for supplication. Philippians 4:6 always challenges me: "Do not worry about anything, but in everything by prayer and supplication with thanksgiving let your requests be made known to God." Is that truth a part of your prayer life? This scripture reminds me not to worry about *anything.* Not my children, not my work, not my future, not my finances, not my church. Nothing! When I'm tempted to worry, I must pray instead! How do I bring my requests to God? If I am to honor this Word, I must always bring my needs to God with thanksgiving. The Holy Spirit is teaching me to do that. By remembering God's faithfulness in the past and being grateful that he hears and answers prayer, I am better able to bring everything to God in prayer with thanksgiving.

The more I walk with the Holy Spirit, the more my requests and supplications in prayer have changed. What do I ask for? For myself, I am always asking God for wisdom and discernment—to see situations and people from God's perspective. I ask for boldness to be a faithful witness of the truth and for transformation—to be changed daily to become more like Christ. When praying for others, I am likely to ask for similar priorities. When praying for physical healing, for example, I am likely to ask God to reveal any hindrances to receiving God's healing grace and for complete healing of body, soul, and spirit.

Questions for Personal Reflection

1. Is your prayer life balanced between adoration, confession, thanksgiving, and supplication?

2. Which area of your prayer life from the A-C-T-S model is the strongest?

3. Which area of your prayer life is the weakest?

4. Consider the requests you are currently bringing to the Lord in prayer. Are you making those requests with thanksgiving?

Activities for Small Groups

1. Practice adoration. Spend five minutes in prayer without asking God for anything. Praise God for who he is. Praise God for his attributes of love, mercy, and holiness.

2. Practice confession. Offer a time of silent confession of sin to God. Then, as people are comfortable, offer a time of confession to one another. As prayers of confession are voiced, the response of the group should be, "In the name of Jesus Christ you are forgiven" (1 Peter 2:9).

3. Practice thanksgiving. Spend five minutes in prayer thanking God for what he does. Consider God's forgiveness, provision, answers to prayer, mighty acts in creation, and gifts of family and friends. Then offer prayers of thanksgiving.

4. Practice supplication. Bring your requests to the Lord.

CHAPTER FOURTEEN

Journaling

Journaling is defined as a record of one's experience with the Lord. It can be a record of our thoughts and feelings about God in much the same way as we might have kept a diary growing up. Journaling can also be a written record of our daily quiet time or it can be a written prayer list with request and answers. Since prayer is a conversation, journaling can be an important tool in remembering and recording the things that God says during our prayer times.

Then the LORD said to Moses, "Write this as a reminder in a book and recite it in the hearing of Joshua." (Exodus 17:14)

Thus says the LORD, the God of Israel: Write in a book all the words that I have spoken to you. (Jeremiah 30:2)

*Then the LORD answered me and said: Write the vision;
make it plain on tablets, so that a runner may read it. For
there is still a vision for the appointed time; it speaks of
the end and does not lie. If it seems to tarry, wait for it; it
will surely come, it will not delay.* (Habakkuk 2:2-3)

The Bible has much to say about journaling. It seems clear
from these scriptures that recording the words of the Lord is
vital. Perhaps God understands better than we do our inability to
remember. Perhaps the Lord wants to build perseverance and
confidence into our prayer life through journaling.

Journaling the word of the Lord as we read scripture serves
as a useful reminder of God's activity in our lives. It is an aid to
remembering God's Word to us. Journaling enables God to apply
the Word to our hearts and lives. If we use a journal like a diary
to record our thoughts and feelings, journaling will require openness, vulnerability, and truthfulness before God.

Scripture speaks often of prophetic words and visions. For
example, Revelation 1:3 says, "Blessed is the one who reads aloud
the words of the prophecy, and blessed are those who hear and
who keep what is written in it; for the time is near." Prophetic
words from the Lord should be written down for later reference.
They may serve as a source of prayer, repentance, or thanksgiving. Remembering a vision given by God is also significant.
Writing down the vision helps us persevere in prayer until that
vision becomes a reality.

How do you get started journaling? Here are some helpful
hints. Choose a journal that is easy to carry, one that is inviting
to use. Date your entries. This will help you look back and reflect
on your daily quiet times. Record your personal insights from
your scripture reading. This exercise will boost your confidence
that God is speaking to you. Provide sufficient time to listen and

record any insights from the Lord. Ask God questions and record his answers. This instruction will reinforce your experience of prayer as a conversation.

Consider writing out your prayers sometimes. You may be amazed how concise your written prayers become. The length of the prayer or flowery language does not matter to God. Rather, God is more concerned about the sincerity of our hearts.

This tool also gives you a measure for how balanced your prayer life really is. Leaving a space for answers to prayer may also be an important part of journaling. Seeing how God answers prayers promotes thanksgiving and may alter what we ask God for in the future.

Every tool for personal prayer should be used under the guidance of the Holy Spirit. Avoid legalism. Pressure or condemnation to write something daily defeats the delight of journaling. Let the Holy Spirit guide you.

I use journaling as a tool in my personal prayer life; however, I still consider myself a beginner. I love keeping a written record because I forget. I can easily forget the promises of God and become discouraged.

I saw the benefits of journaling with my prayer partner long before I ever began to journal myself. Years ago I had a prayer partner who frequently kept a written record of our corporate prayer times. It was revealing to look back at the things we had prayed together and see how God had answered our prayers. It was during these early experiences that I first encountered prophetic words from the Lord, and I felt an urgency to remember what God had said. Journaling helps us recognize and remember prophetic words.

In order to journal for myself, I had to honestly overcome some personal stumbling blocks. My hindrances were perfectionism, legalism, and comparison with others that resulted in guilt. Since my friend had been such an avid *journaler*, my natural tendency was to let Carol do it. Since I didn't feel I could do it as well as she did, my first inclination was to not do it at all. I've come to understand that is perfectionism. When I was honest with God about the stumbling blocks to journaling on my own, God brought healing and release from guilt.

I began journaling when I was given my first journal as a gift. I wanted to honor my friend's gift and decided to use it. When I opened the book, I was delighted to find that the pages were not blank. The book was inviting and had scripture quotations and pictures as well as space to write. Since I didn't feel the pressure to fill entirely blank pages, I began easily. And I have continued to use journaling regularly at different seasons of my life. I attempt to allow the Holy Spirit to guide me because he knows best when journaling should be my priority.

Journaling really does require openness, vulnerability, and truthfulness before God. For myself, I had to get past the fear that someone else might read my journal. However, privacy is still an issue. I believe you should be the one to decide what gets shared with others. I believe in expressing my true feelings to God and journaling is a tool to work through feelings honestly. Because I have a tendency toward perfectionism, I have to give myself permission to write any way I want. I'm learning not to edit myself, when I journal.

Jeremiah 36:2 says to write "all the words that I have spoken to you." That is my primary source of journaling at this time. During our *Aldersgate* national conference, for example, we are careful to record all the prophetic words given by the Lord. We ask God to "put [his] laws in [our] minds, and write them on [our] hearts" (Hebrews 8:10). These become a source of prayer and encouragement for our ARM intercessors. (ARM has a nationwide network of prayer warriors that consistently uplift the ministry and pray for the renewal of the church. Contact ARM to find out more about the intercessors network.)

God often speaks to me through visions. I've come to understand the importance of remembering these visions and holding
them before the Lord until they become a reality. I identify with
Habakkuk 2:3 when it says, "For there is still a vision for the
appointed time; it speaks of the end, and does not lie. If it seems
to tarry, wait for it; it will surely come, it will not delay." God has
an appointed time for every vision to become a reality. God may
seem to tarry, but his timing is always perfect. Journaling helps
me remember this truth.

God gave me a specific vision of my mother's salvation.
During a very difficult time, God showed me clearly that her salvation would be accomplished. However, it was eighteen long
years between the time God gave me that vision and it became
a reality. Was I tempted to become discouraged? Yes, indeed.
However, recording and remembering that vision helped me
overcome discouragement as I waited. It increased my faith and
was a wonderful source of thanksgiving when my mother finally
received Christ as her personal Savior.

God also wants us to record our visions so that we can share
them with others. Do you remember the vision of the stones that
God gave me when I first became National Prayer Coordinator
for Aldersgate Renewal Ministries? (See page 78.) I knew from
this vision that the Lord would raise up intercessors with a God-
given burden to pray. My part was simply to encourage people to
ask the Lord, "Which stone is yours to carry?" I have been able
to share that vision with others, and I know that it is a continu-
ing source of encouragement as intercessors are called to pray for
ARM and for the renewal of the church.

Questions for Personal Reflection

1. Did you keep a diary growing up? If so, was it a rewarding
    experience? Did you struggle with others reading your diary?

2. Is journaling a part of your current prayer life? Do you use journaling on a regular basis or at different seasons of your life?

3. Do you identify with legalism, perfectionism or comparison as stumbling blocks to using the tool of journaling?

4. Do you have a means to record the things God says in prayer? Have you considered using a computer as a journal? Have you had opportunity to share these words with others? How were they received?

5. Consider the following model for journaling. Choose any scripture that the Lord brings to mind.

   - My Reflections on Scripture Reading
   - My Prayer
   - My Question: Lord, what area of my prayer life do you want me to focus on today?

Activities for Small Groups

1. Pray as a group for one another to be led by the Holy Spirit to apply this teaching on journaling to your personal prayer life.

2. Experiment with keeping a journal of your corporate prayer requests and answers to prayer.

3. Record the prophetic words and visions that God gives you during your corporate times of prayer.

CHAPTER FIFTEEN

Daily Quiet Time

While every tool for personal prayer in this unit is important, daily quiet time likely ranks as a first priority if we are to grow in our personal prayer life. Daily quiet time is defined as a time set aside every day to nurture our relationship with God. We need to remind ourselves that our purpose is not just to study scripture, to read devotions, or to pray. We spend this time alone with God to nurture our relationship with him.

Perhaps the biggest downfall of a daily quiet time is not encountering God. We can get caught in the trap of *going through the motions* and never really experience God. We'll look honestly at some helps for having and sustaining personal time with the Lord.

In the morning, while it was still very dark, he got up and went out to a deserted place, and there he prayed. (Mark 1:35)

Now during those days he went out to the mountain to pray; and he spent the night in prayer to God. (Luke 6:12)

But he would withdraw to deserted places and pray. (Luke 5:16)

———————————

Jesus is our best model of one who consistently spent time alone with the Father. As we noted in "Lessons from the Prayer Life of Jesus," scriptures indicate that Jesus had a pattern of withdrawal from others to intentionally spend time alone with God. Despite the busyness of ministry, Jesus made daily quiet time a priority. He made use of every time of day from beginning to end. The scriptures indicate that Jesus prayed very early in the morning, but he also spent the night in prayer. The most important element appears to be time alone with God

If Jesus needed this undivided time alone with God, how much more must we need this important tool in our personal prayer life? Our daily quiet time is a reflection of our relationship with Jesus. What does your daily quiet time say about your relationship with Jesus? Just as we suffer physically if we miss too many meals, we suffer spiritually if we miss the rich refreshment and nourishment that comes with our times alone with God.

All relationships require time and effort. We know that is true in marriage, in our relationships with our children, and in our friendships with others. Prayer is a relationship that also requires time and attention. Like the vine and the branches in John 15, we need to be certain that we gain our spiritual nourishment from Christ.

All of us are looking for helps for a daily quiet time. On some level, we all want to nurture our relationship with Christ, but the demands of life often cause us to stumble. First of all, pick a time that's best for you. For many of us, that is first thing in the morning, before the demands of daily life crowd out our time with the Lord. Some of us are not morning people, no matter how much we'd like to be. So praying at another time remains an option. God deserves our best, the *first fruits* of our time. So finding an appropriate time is the first priority.

There are a wide variety of helps for daily quiet time. There are daily devotionals and many Bible reading programs available. Lack of material is never the problem. Choose one and get started. Using a variety of resources keeps your experience with the Lord fresh. Try one for a season and then use another or none at all. Just meet with God.

For most of us, daily quiet time is something we have tried and failed, I fit that category, so staying on track is the real issue. I am convinced that no amount of guilt or condemnation will motivate us. Instead, knowing the grace of God for our failures and his desire to be in communion with us will help us stay the course.

By personality, I am an introvert. I truly value time alone, and I gain energy from being alone. I love people, but I am not an extrovert and being with people does not build my energy like it does for some. Therefore, I think I have an easier time sustaining a daily quiet time. I love quiet.

Why does daily quiet time matter for me? I am convinced that John 15:5 is true: "Apart from me you can do nothing." Daily quiet time is necessary for me as a time to surrender my will to God. My biggest hurdles are self-centeredness and pride. Effort in the flesh is a daily temptation. One of my biggest fears is walking in the flesh rather than the Spirit. The Lord is teaching me that I must bring my strengths to God daily. I seem better able to bring my weaknesses to the Lord in prayer and be dependent on him totally in those areas. However, surrendering those things that I perceive to be my strengths is my greatest area of need. I must die daily to my own agenda.

What is my daily quiet time like? I use a variety of helps for Bible reading and devotionals. At different seasons of my life, one seems to be more helpful than others. But my daily quiet time is not primarily study time or even intercessory prayer time. My primary focus is quiet. My purpose is to encounter God and wait on him. I spend much time listening and praying with the Spirit.

Since by nature I am not an early riser, I spent too much time condemning myself for not being able to rise early "in the morning, while it [is] still very dark" (Mark 1:35) to pray. Instead, I now begin my day with praise. Even before I get out of bed, I intentionally spend a few minutes connecting with God in praise. Then I begin my day and God carves out time for me to spend alone with him. It is the cry of my heart to honor God with time alone with him, and God has consistently answered that prayer.

Questions for Personal Reflection

1. Do you currently have a daily quiet time? What has been your biggest stumbling block to a consistent time with the Lord?

2. What does your daily quiet time look like?

3. Are you encountering God or just *going through the motions* of a daily quiet time?

4. What do you need to do to strengthen or begin a daily time with the Lord?

5. Try this personal quiet time activity. Read Psalm 1 twice. The first time, read the entire Psalm to be familiar with its content. The second time, read the Psalm prayerfully asking God to speak to your heart. Stop and meditate on any verse that stands out to you. Listen for what the Lord is saying to you personally.

Activities for Small Groups

1. Discuss with your group how guilt or condemnation may have hindered your efforts to have a consistent daily quiet time. Pray for one another to be set free from any bondages of the enemy.

2. Discuss with your group how you might covenant with one another to keep a daily quiet time. Pray for one another to begin or strengthen a daily quiet time with the Lord.

3. Pray 1 Thessalonians 5:23-24 over the group: "May the God of peace himself sanctify you entirely; and may your spirit and soul and body be kept sound and blameless at the coming of our Lord Jesus Christ. The one who calls you is faithful, and he will do this."

The Promise of Intimacy with God in Prayer

This picture depicts a believer's journey to know intimacy with God in prayer. On one side of the wall is the manifest glory of God. On the other side is a believer attempting to walk in intimacy with God. Written on the wall are examples of obstacles or hindrances to knowing God intimately. Who built the wall? Certainly not God. We build the wall between God and us. Unfortunately, we can't get around the wall, over the wall, or under the wall. But the good news is that God can demolish the walls of separation. This unit will look at some of the obstacles and the remedies for walking in intimacy with God. Together let's trust that God will be at work to reveal and to heal anything that could stand in the way of our experiencing intimacy with God in prayer.

CHAPTER SIXTEEN

The Promise Is for You

God desires intimacy with us! Prayer that is from the heart opens the door for us to experience God in deep and personal ways. Prayer can and should be heart to heart conversations.

Scripture shows us that God always desired intimacy. Consider Genesis 2:7. Creation required God to be up close and personal. God put his mouth to Adam's nostrils and breathed life into him. God could have chosen to create human beings from a distance, but he didn't. He chose a very intimate means to bring life.

Then the LORD God formed man from the dust of the ground, and breathed into his nostrils the breath of life; and the man became a living being. (Genesis 2:7)

They heard the sound of the Lord God walking in the garden at the time of the evening breeze, and the man and his

> *wife hid themselves from the presence of the Lord God*
> *among the trees of the garden. But the Lord God called*
> *to the man, and said to him, "Where are you?"* (Genesis
> 3:8-9)

God continued this intimacy with Adam in the Garden of Eden. Adam enjoyed fellowship with God in the cool of the evening as they walked and talked together. But that intimacy lasted only for a time. Then sin entered the picture. In Genesis 3:8-9 the relationship that began in intimacy was destroyed through sin. The story of Adam and Eve is *good news, bad news, good news.* The good news is that man's relationship with God began in intimacy. That was always God's priority. The bad news is sin destroyed that relationship. Man would be expelled from God's presence. The final good news is intimacy can be restored through Christ. Hear the invitation to intimacy in these scriptures. Even though God knew Adam's sin, God was still calling out to Adam, "Where are you?" That is the call of God today. "Where are you, beloved? Come to me." From Genesis to Revelation the invitation stands. "The Spirit and the bride say, 'Come.' And let everyone who hears say, 'Come'" (Revelation 22:17a). Will you come?

> *"I will take you as my people, and I will be your God. You*
> *shall* know *that I am the* LORD *your God, who has freed*
> *you from the burdens of the Egyptians."* (Exodus 6:7,
> emphasis added)

In the Old Testament God chose the Israelites as his own covenant people. He designated the prophets and the priests to represent the people before God. God spoke to the prophets and they related God's message to the people. God gave laws and rituals for the priests to make atonement for the people. The common people of the day did not know God intimately. Instead, they relied on the experiences of a few designated leaders to know God.

Yada means to know intimately. This Hebrew word is not representative of head knowledge. It means knowing God from personal experience and has the connotation of seeing for yourself. Consider Exodus 6:7. The Israelites were promised that they would *know* that God had freed them from the Egyptians. That is the kind of intimacy God promises each of us. We can know God.

Thus the LORD *used to speak to Moses face to face, as one speaks to a friend.* (Exodus 33:11)

Whenever Moses went out to the tent, all the people would rise and stand, each of them, at the entrance of their tents and watch Moses until he had gone into the tent. (Exodus 33:8)

Abraham and Moses are examples of people from the Old Testament who knew God intimately. Consider Exodus 33:11. From direct experience, Moses encountered God in the tent of meeting. Moses spoke to God face to face. What did the people do when Moses went to meet with God? They stood at their tents and watched Moses enter God's presence. They were spectators rather than ones who experienced God. That is a lesson for each of us. We can choose to be spectators, or we can choose to experience God.

Abraham also modeled intimacy with God. Genesis 17, for example, chronicles an encounter Abram had with the Lord when he was ninety-nine. The Lord said, "I am God Almighty; walk before me, and be blameless" (Genesis 17:1). God changed Abram's name to Abraham and made a covenant with him to be the ancestor of a multitude of nations.

In the New Testament, God invites everyone to be intimate with him. Through the covenant made in Jesus' blood, all individuals are invited into an intimate relationship with him. When Jesus died on the cross, the curtain in the temple was torn from top to bottom (Luke 23:45). Meditate for a moment on the significance of this tear in the temple's curtain. It was not torn by human effort. God did that to demonstrate that Jesus' death made a way from us to freely enter into God's presence. All barriers were broken down. Consider Hebrews 10:19-22:

> Therefore, my friends, since we have confidence to enter the sanctuary by the blood of Jesus, by the new and living way that he opened for us through the curtain (that is, through his flesh), and since we have a great priest over the house of God, let us approach with a true heart in full assurance of faith, with our hearts sprinkled clean from an evil conscience and our bodies washed with pure water.

Jesus' sacrifice opened the way for all to freely enter into God's presence. Will you respond to the invitation?

I have struggled personally to believe God's promise of intimacy with him through prayer. I understood God's promises with my head long before I experienced that intimacy in my life. I believed intimacy was possible for the body of Christ long before I believed it was possible for *me*. I needed to come to grips with the obstacles and hindrances that stood in my way. I needed to understand God had provided the remedy for every piece of the wall I had built that separated me from God. My journey was probably not unlike yours. Healing and restoration is for you and for me. That's the good news of the gospel.

Questions for Personal Reflection

1. Even the word *intimacy* may be difficult for some. Victims of sexual or physical abuse, for example, may find that term difficult to think about in their relationship with God. What other words could be substituted for *intimacy* in this discussion?

2. When you consider your current prayer life, what barriers do you discern between yourself and God?

3. Do you want to speak to God *face to face* as Moses did? Why or why not?

4. Do you identify with the spectators in the crowd or with Moses in Exodus 33?

Activities for Small Groups

1. Spend some time thanking God for the sacrifice of Christ on the cross that opened the way for all to know intimacy with God.

2. Pray for each other that you will remain open to the direction of the Holy Spirit as you look at obstacles and hindrances to closeness with God.

3. Pray Jeremiah 31:3 for a partner. "I have loved you (insert name) with an everlasting love; therefore I have continued my faithfulness to you."

CHAPTER SEVENTEEN

Overcoming Obstacles to Intimacy with God

One definition of intimacy that may prove helpful is "to know fully and to love completely." God knows us fully and still loves us completely. That's amazing, but true. Jesus is the source and the provision for intimacy with God through prayer. With that wonderful promise of intimacy in mind, we need to deal with those things that cause us to stumble in our desire to walk in closeness with God.

In this chapter we'll look at unconfessed sin, unforgiveness, and disappointment. Each of these issues can build a wall between God and us. However, we'll put special emphasis on the remedies God provides for us to overcome these obstacles. There is a remedy!

Unconfessed sin is sin that God has revealed to you but you have not dealt with. Perhaps your response has been denial or rebellion to God's promptings. Examples of unconfessed sin may be disobedience, selfishness, pride, or many other things. Unconfessed sin becomes entrenched in our lives with each refusal to deal with it.

But the LORD *God called to the man, and said to him, "Where are you?" He said, "I heard the sound of you in the garden, and I was afraid, because I was naked; and I hid myself." He said, "Who told you that you were naked? Have you eaten from the tree of which I commanded you not to eat?" The man said, "The woman whom you gave to be with me, she gave me fruit from the tree, and I ate." Then the* LORD *God said to the woman, "What is this you have done?" The woman said, "The serpent tricked me, and I ate."* (Genesis 3:9-13)

Why is unconfessed sin so important? Repeated unconfessed sin causes our heart to grow cold. It results in evil desires, stubborn pride, and hatefulness. Sin that is not dealt with opens the door for the enemy. Unconfessed sin can seriously hinder our prayer life by allowing the enemy a foothold in our lives. God will appear to become distant and silent during prayer. The wall of separation is built stone by stone, day by day.

Earlier we looked at Adam and Eve. Consider again Genesis 3:9-13. When God confronted them, Adam and Eve resorted to hiding and passing blame. Their unconfessed sin resulted in broken relationships, a fallen world, and expulsion from the Garden. Down through the ages, men and women have continued to deal with sin by denial, by hiding, and by passing blame.

There is a remedy. The remedy for unconfessed sin is confession and repentance. Confession can simply be defined as agreeing with God. It means to be willing to call sin, *sin*. It is not a moral failure or a mistake; it is sin. Consider 1 John 1:8-9. If we say we are without sin, we deceive ourselves. Confession is not denying sin or hiding or passing blame. When we confess our sins before God, we take accountability for our sins. Then we can cast ourselves on the mercy and faithfulness of God and trust that he will indeed forgive our sins and cleanse us from all unrighteousness. Is there malice, insincerity, envy or slander in your life? God wants to deal with those sins that stand in the way of intimacy with him.

If we say that we have no sin, we deceive ourselves, and the truth is not in us. If we confess our sins, he who is faithful and just will forgive us our sins and cleanse us from all unrighteousness. (1 John 1:8-9)

Rid yourself, therefore, of all malice, and all guile, insincerity, envy, and all slander. (1 Peter 2:1)

Confession of sin is only part of the remedy. We dare not stop short with just recognizing the sin. The complete remedy includes repentance. Repentance is not just being sorry we got caught in sin, but requires a conscious choice to turn away from our sin. It is a *180-degree turn* that transforms our lives and sets us in a totally new direction. Repentance brings hope and healing and is what God requires, but he is the source for true repentance. "The sacrifice acceptable to God is a broken spirit; a broken and contrite heart, O God, you will not despise" (Psalm 51:17). We can trust God's faithfulness when we repent from the heart.

I have several examples of times in my life when I allowed unconfessed sin to fester and build a wall between God and me. None of them are pretty stories. Sin is real and has definite consequences. I remember a time when God specifically dealt with me about lying in my life. My family of origin practiced different types of lying. Deception and white lies were part of my learned behavior growing up. If it caused you to look better or to get ahead, these behaviors were acceptable and even valued. Such is the way in many non-Christian households like mine. But, perhaps Christian households can also fall prey to this type of deception. When I came to know Christ, my lying behaviors were not the first thing God dealt with. In his grace and mercy, however, God brought me to a place where I came face to face with my lying. God told me to confess that sin to others and make restitution. At that moment, I made a choice. I said to God, "That's too hard. I can't do that." Because of my unconfessed sin, a wall began to be built. I was in agony in my relationship with God. God felt distant and unapproachable. Thankfully, God broke through to me, and I realized that confession and repentance were the only answer. I confessed my sin to God and repented of my lying behavior. I confessed my sin to those I had hurt. I also made public restitution for my sin. I'm not sure that God always requires this final step, but he gave me specific direction to make restitution and I obeyed. Oh what freedom, friends, as that wall came tumbling down.

I learned a hard lesson that day and I believe that experience has taught me to deal with sin radically in my life. Now, for example, when I see judgementalism in my life I am more likely to confess that sin immediately. In addition, I have found that the accountability of confessing my sins to other trusted believers brings much freedom and joy as they pray with me to see those walls of division crumbled in the power of the Holy Spirit.

Unforgiveness is another obstacle to intimacy with God. Unforgiveness is simply a failure to forgive. It leads to grudges, hatred, bitterness, avoidance, and even a desire for revenge. Unforgiveness becomes entrenched with every thought as we continue to entertain thoughts of revenge or bitterness. We often play the memory of the offense over and over in our minds. If we have unforgiveness toward others, we will have a break in intimacy with God. Unforgiveness is like a cancer that eats away at our relationship with God and with others. The only remedy is forgiveness.

Put away from you all bitterness and wrath and anger and wrangling and slander, together with all malice, and be kind to one another, tenderhearted, forgiving one another, as God in Christ has forgiven you. (Ephesians 4:31-32)

"Then his lord summoned him and said to him, 'You wicked slave! I forgave you all that debt because you pleaded with me. Should you not have had mercy on your fellow slave, as I had mercy on you?'" (Matthew 18:32-33)

"Whenever you stand praying, forgive, if you have anything against anyone; so that your Father in heaven may also forgive you your trespasses." (Mark 11:25)

Forgiveness means to give up resentment against or the desire to punish, to stop being angry with, to pardon, or to cancel a debt. Forgiveness can be used as a legal term for the cancellation of debt. If the demands of the law are not met, you remain in debt morally to holy God. Forgiveness cancels that debt and sets us free.

There is much confusion, even in the body of Christ, as to what forgiveness is and what it is not. Here are some guidelines for what forgiveness is not:

- Forgiveness is not in human nature. But it is in divine nature, and we partake of it as children of God. God forgives us; therefore, we can forgive others by the power of the Holy Spirit.

- Forgiveness is not numbing ourselves and ignoring the offense. Instead, we come face to face with the sin and deal openly with it.

- Forgiveness is not a feeling, but a decision and a process. If we wait to forgive until we feel like it, forgiveness will never happen. Forgiveness is a choice we make in response to God's Word. It is also a process that takes time and attention to each level of forgiveness. We must deal with forgiveness of the one who offended us, forgiveness related to God, and forgiveness of ourselves. Each level of forgiveness is an important part of the process.

- Forgiveness is not the healing, but it is an essential step that leads to it. Forgiveness can be seen as *doing surgery on an infected wound*. Forgiveness lances the wound and the bitterness and resentment begins to be drained out of our lives. When we walk through the three levels of forgiveness described above, the healing is still not complete. The next step usually involves prayers for inner healing, the healing of memories. Unfortunately, this step is often overlooked. The good news is God can walk back into the hurtful, painful memories of our past and bring healing.

- Forgiveness is not the immediate reestablishment of trust. This is one area where the enemy often deceives us. When we have done our part to forgive, there is no guarantee that the relationship will be restored. In fact, it may not be. The outcome of the relationship is dependent on the response of the other person. Whether or not trust is reestablished does not mean forgiveness has not taken place.

- Forgiveness is not easy. Christ requires it and he is the
  provision for it. Page 124 lists only a few of the many
  scriptures that deal with God's view of forgiveness.
  Ephesians 4 is God's command to forgive as Christ has
  forgiven you. When we understand the lavish forgiveness
  of Christ, we can more fully deal with our need to forgive others.

My own story contains many examples of hard lessons
learned about unforgiveness. I held many misconceptions about
what forgiveness really was. I have come to understand that
unforgiveness is not an option for Christians. We must forgive.
Working through the inner healing of memories that has been so
much a part of my life, required that I learn forgiveness. As I
sought to walk through the three levels of forgiveness from others, God, and myself, I often stumbled on the part of forgiving
myself. Perhaps, because of my perfectionist tendencies, I still
find it hard to forgive myself. I know it is essential to healing, so
I am learning, by God's grace, to make that choice.

Unforgiveness is also an issue in my relationship with other
Christians. I tend to hold Christians to a higher standard and find
that I need to forgive them even more often than non-Christians.
My experience is that I don't find non-Christians to be always
loving and kind. I believe that is impossible outside of Christ.
But, I tend to expect that standard for Christians and must deal
with personal disappointment and unforgiveness often.

Disappointment is also an obstacle to intimacy with God.
Disappointment means a person or thing that fails to satisfy the
hopes or expectations of another; that which leaves a person
unsatisfied or frustrated. Dealing with disappointment also
involves three levels: disappointment with God, with others, and
with ourselves.

Disappointment with God sometimes occurs because of assumptions we make that he will give us our desires that are not yet conformed to his desires. The results of disappointment with God may be loss of enthusiasm for prayer, fear of rejection, or a halt in our spiritual growth. We turn away from God in disappointment because we perceive that he has not met our needs. The remedy for this level of disappointment involves a biblical understanding of the security we have in God's love for us through Jesus and his death on the cross for us. We must come to the true knowledge that God always works for our best. God has good reasons for saying *wait* or *no* in answer to some of our requests in prayer.

There is also disappointment with others because they fail, or we perceive that they have failed us in some way. The remedy for disappointment at this level involves receiving and extending forgiveness. "In the name of Jesus you are forgiven," is a powerful declaration of truth that shatters the wall of disappointment in our relationships with others. It comes often at the cost of accepting others and accepting ourselves.

The third level of forgiveness involves disappointment with ourselves. Sometimes we fail to accept our own humanity and God's provision for it in Christ. We can be our own worst enemy. The remedy for disappointment with ourselves involves a growing understanding of God's character and his ways. When we know that God is not disappointed in us, that he truly loves and forgives us, we can more easily deal with disappointment with ourselves.

My story also contains strongholds of disappointment with others, with God, and especially with myself. One example, that included all three levels of disappointment, occurred when my youngest son fathered a child out of wedlock. I experienced disappointment with my son who had been called into the ministry and was pursing his first semester in college toward that goal. I was disappointed and angry with God for not preventing the unplanned pregnancy, dealt with disappointment, and blamed myself. "Where had I failed my son?" The healing was a decision and a process. In God's timing and mercy, he dealt with each level of disappointment. I would not trade the wonderful lesson of God's grace that I learned during that most painful period. The wall of separation that could have damaged my relationship with God was shattered by his grace.

Questions for Personal Reflection

1. Spend some time in personal reflection and journal your answers to these questions about unconfessed sin.

   - Is there one area of sin that has blocked or hindered my relationship with God?
   - How have others been affected or hurt by my sin?
   - Has sin harmed my own life?
   - How should I obtain forgiveness from those I hurt by this sin?
   - Is restitution possible?
   - Repent from the habit or lifestyle of these hindrances.
   - Seek the Lord's full cleansing and restoration.

2. Ask God to reveal and heal any areas of unforgiveness.

3. Seek healing from the Lord for obstacles of disappointment that may hinder your intimacy with God in prayer.

Activities for Small Groups

1. Read James 5:13: "Are any among you suffering? They should pray. Are any cheerful? They should sing songs of praise. Are any among you sick? They should call for the elders of the church and have them pray over them, anointing them with oil in the name of the Lord. The prayer of faith will save the

sick and the Lord will raise them up; and anyone who has committed sins will be forgiven." Use this scripture as a basis for sharing and prayer for each other as you ask God to reveal and heal obstacles to intimacy with God in prayer.

2. Pray Isaiah 11:2-3 for a partner:

> The spirit of the LORD shall rest on (insert name), the spirit of wisdom and understanding, the spirit of counsel and might, the spirit of knowledge and the fear of the LORD. (insert name)'s delight shall be in the fear of the LORD.

CHAPTER EIGHTEEN

Breaking Barriers
to Intimacy with God

When you look into the mirror of God's Word, what picture of God the Father do you see? Does your picture of God line up with the scriptures? Many of us have distorted images of God. Distorted means twisted or out of shape, changed from the usual or normal. These distorted images of God cause harm. How we think about God dramatically affects our prayer life and our ability to walk in intimacy with him.

Distorted images of God are set in place very early in life. We take the limited picture of an authority figure in our earthly life and transfer that image to our belief about God. These authority figures are often father, mother, grandfather, grandmother, or even a trusted teacher or a coach. If your earthly father was judgmental and critical, for example, it is easy to transfer those characteristics to God, your heavenly Father.

Distorted images of God are also set in place by judgments and vows. Briefly, a judgment is something someone else says about you. Statements like, "You always mess up; you'll never amount to anything; you're ugly; you're terrible in math," are examples of judgments made against a person. These statements can become truth in our minds if they are repeated often enough. We begin to live according to the judgments made against us.

Vows are something we say about ourselves. We begin to believe the judgments made against us and internalize them as truth. Then we make statements like, "I'm a screw up; I'll never be any good; or I'll never trust people again." These vows have a definite affect on how we see God and relate to him.

Ask God to help you identify any distortions of his true character. You may lack the conviction that God is always good, for example, or believe that God fails to forgive and holds grudges like some people. Remember that there is a remedy for every barrier to intimacy with God. Seek the Lord for complete healing.

Thus says the LORD: *Do not let the wise boast in their wisdom, do not let the mighty boast in their might, do not let the wealthy boast in their wealth; but let those who boast boast in this, that they understand me, that I am the* LORD; *I act with steadfast love, justice, and righteousness in the earth, for in these things I delight, says the* LORD. (Jeremiah 9:23-24)

What God declares about himself is the best medicine for distorted images of God. Consider Jeremiah 9:23-24. This is one of many scriptures that declare the true character of God. Ask yourself these questions: Do I consistently believe and act on these truths about God? Do I trust that God always acts in steadfast love, justice, and righteousness?

Apparently, most people don't believe that about God. There is a familiar saying in many congregations. We repeat often, "God is good . . . all the time." And the answer is "All the time, God is good." If you analyze this statement, you may find many people who attend church do not truly believe that God is *always* good. They have a distorted image of God.

Watch how people react when bad things happen to good people. That is when you really find out what people think about God. How do you know if a distortion applies to your life? Consider how you react to circumstances. Often our reactions show evidence of past trauma that have led to unhealthy images of God. What would cause only a minor reaction for the average person, causes a major problem for the person with a distorted image of God. The circumstance *touches a nerve* that is unhealed, and our reaction is often blown out of proportion.

"Come to me, all you that are weary and are carrying heavy burdens, and I will give you rest. Take my yoke upon you, and learn from me; for I am gentle and humble in heart, and you will find rest for your souls."
(Matthew 11:28-29)

Distorted images of God also affect our prayer life. These misconceptions will cause us to avoid God. We put God off or hold him at arms length. In avoidance, we miss out on God's love and guidance. We are unable, for example, to appropriate the promise of Matthew 11:28-29. Sadly, the rest and peace God desires for our mind and heart escapes us.

My past contained many distorted images of God that needed healing. Have you ever said, "You want me to do what

God? I can't do that; that's too hard." I have. I determined that God was too demanding. Have you ever complained to God, "God, that's not fair! Why God?" That's evidence of an unhealthy view of God.

I think the distortion that has most deeply affected my life is God is a critical parent or a condemning judge. I want to share part of my story to offer hope and healing to others who may have encountered this distortion of God. I do not share my story to place blame. In fact, the only reason I can share my story is because God has done much healing. Both my mother and my father are deceased and for most of my life, my parents were non-Christians. My mother accepted Christ as her personal Savior before she died. Both my parents loved and provided for me. In many ways my life was normal. I've come to understand that the unconditional love I needed and desired from my parents can only be found in Christ.

I was never physically or sexually abused, but verbal abuse can be very devastating. My earthly father was very critical and condemning. I got the message loud and clear that I didn't measure up. I had real problems with rejection and low self-esteem. I became performance oriented. As a perfectionist, I was always trying to jump through hoops to find love and acceptance. I never felt I received unconditional love. Conditional love says, "I'll love you if . . . I'll love you when . . ." That kind of love is always based on performance. It promotes restlessness and striving.

I held God at arms length. There were times when I would run to God with a true desire for intimacy, but always seemed to shrink back with feelings of shame and guilt. Why would I want to be close to a God who I felt, even unconsciously, was like a critical parent? There was a constant push and pull in my prayer life. At some level, I believed freedom and intimacy were possible, but I did not experience that in prayer.

God brought healing in my life through several means. First of all, God enabled me to saturate myself in the Word. I studied God's character as revealed in the Bible. A study of the names of God from scripture was particularly helpful to me. I love *El Ro'i* found in Genesis 16:13. That name of God means "the Strong One who sees." For a long time, that was not my picture of God. I found healing in believing that God saw my circumstances, knew my pain, and really did care for me. Demolishing the lies of the enemy and building the truth of God changes the distortions we once believed.

Healing also came through strong, biblical teaching and experience of inner healing. The truth is God can reach back into those unhealed memories that are the root cause of the distorted images of God. Combined with inner healing, deliverance from spirits of trauma like fear, guilt, and shame may also be necessary.

One example of prayers for inner healing from my own life may encourage others to seek prayer. I always knew that I had a problem with rejection. I thought God rejected me, and I was sure other people rejected me. Yet, I did not know the root cause of the problem until God revealed a memory from my past that needed healing. In the memory, I was a small child of three or four years of age. I was curled up on the floor screaming, "I'm so sorry. I promise I'll never do it again." My mother, in her brokenness, had some unhealthy forms of discipline. In the memory, my mother was pretending to call the local orphanage and saying something like this: "Margie's been bad. I don't want her any more. Please come take her away." God showed me that this incident was the open door for the spirit of rejection and one of the causes of my distorted image of God. I walked through the prayers for forgiveness outlined in the last chapter. I made a decision to forgive my mother. I admitted my anger toward God and asked for forgiveness. I also made the choice to forgive myself. Even at the young age of three or four I had internalized that the incident was my fault. Maybe if I had *tried a little harder, been a little better* this would not have happened. I'm thankful for the healing and deliverance I received that day. I also know that inner healing is a process. I'd like to tell you that praying that prayer one day solved all my problems. It did not. There were other memories and other needs for healing revealed. Nevertheless, the process of praying for inner healing has remained a faithful tool in my prayer life. I have also been blessed to be a blessing. God provides many opportunities to pray with others for inner healing and deliverance. Praise the Lord!

As you pursue healing, remember that God also uses professional/Christian counseling to aid inner healing. The healing is often a process that involves many different resources, but the rewards are great.

Unbelief is another barrier to intimacy with God. Unbelief means a withholding or lack of belief, especially in religion or certain religious doctrines. Before we come to know Christ personally, each of us was in a stronghold of unbelief. We did not believe the promises of God. Furthermore, Christians can also easily fall prey to unbelief.

Take care, brothers and sisters, that none of you may have an evil, unbelieving heart that turns away from the living God. But exhort one another every day, as long as it is called "today," so that none of you may be hardened by the deceitfulness of sin. (Hebrews 3:12-13)

Unbelief affects our prayer life. It is seemingly innocent, yet this sin underlies them all. Unbelief leads to rebellion, even subtly, and wayward hardened hearts. Our unbelief will cause us to doubt that God wants to be close to us or to bless us. Hebrews

3:12-13 contains a serious warning about unbelief. Beware of an, "evil, unbelieving heart," that will cause us to turn away from God. Faced with choices every day, we can choose to turn toward God or away from God at any time. Unbelief causes our heart to be hardened by the deceitfulness of sin. Often we will not see our heart becoming hard with unbelief until we are well down that destructive road.

The remedy for unbelief is recognition of sin, followed by confession and repentance. First, we must see our own unbelief. Then, we must call unbelief sin and confess that openly to the Lord. Finally, we must choose to turn away from unbelief and return to faith in God and his promises.

The story of the father who brings his demon possessed son to Jesus for healing in Mark 9 offers us a scriptural guideline for overcoming unbelief. The father's response to Jesus in Mark 9:24 is "I believe; help my unbelief!" That is a powerful prayer that God hears and responds to.

My own story contains instances of unbelief. Personally, I find it easier to believe the promises of God for other people rather than for myself. I've come to understand that this is unbelief, and I'm learning to break that stronghold.

I also recognize that the exercise of spiritual gifts requires faith. Romans 12:6, for example, speaks about the gift of prophecy: "We have gifts that differ according to the grace given us; prophesy, in proportion to faith." Unbelief can hinder the proper use of spiritual gifts. It can cause us to doubt whether God is really speaking to us prophetically and may hinder us from exercising that gift in the body of Christ. Do you want to exercise the spiritual gifts in faith? Ask God to reveal any strongholds of unbelief. Each time God reveals a stronghold of unbelief, I have cried out to God in prayer. The answer has been true to God's Word. "I believe, help my unbelief," has always brought healing and freedom.

Romans 4:20-21 speaks about the faith of Abraham. It is a model for how I want to live my life. Can God say about you and me that we are, *"fully persuaded* that God [has the] power to do what he had promised" (NIV, italics added)? I am trusting God to make that truth a reality in my life. How about you? Ask God to shatter any stronghold of unbelief.

Questions for Personal Reflection

1. What are the distorted images of God with which you have struggled? Do you think you know why?

2. In Jeremiah 9:23-24 God says if we boast we are to boast that we understand and know God. How do you think we can do that? Do you want to? Is there anything keeping you from it?

3. In looking at the scriptures regarding unbelief, were there any words or thoughts that surprised you? How can these words from scripture be applied to your life?

Activities for Small Groups

1. Pray for one another to be healed from any distorted images of God. Here are some guidelines for inner healing prayer.

   - Recall the event: Ask God to show you the root cause of the problem. Remember that the root cause my not be revealed in one prayer setting, but may be disclosed over a period of time.
   - Forgive the person responsible.
   - Forgive God: God has not sinned, but you may hold a perceived grievance against God.
   - Forgive yourself.
   - Ask Jesus to walk into the situation with you: The truth is God was there. Pray, "Lord, where were you?" Then wait expectantly and watch in silent prayer.

2. Pray for unbelief to be revealed and healed in your lives.

3. Pray the blessing of Romans 4:20-21 with a partner. (Insert name) does not waver through unbelief. He or she is strengthened in faith and gives glory to God. (Insert name) is fully persuaded that God has the power to do what he has promised.

References

Adams, Lucy. 1998. *Song Stories*. Cookeville, TN: J. Platinum Printing.

Bryant, Charles V. 1991. *Rediscovering Our Spiritual Gifts*. Nashville, TN: Upper Room Books.

Smith, William. 1962. *Smith's Bible Dictionary*. Nashville, TN: Thomas Nelson Publishers.

Bibliography

Adams, Lucy. *52 Hymn Story Devotions*. Nashville, TN: Abingdon, 2000.

Book of United Methodist Worship, The United Methodist Hymnal, Nashville, TN: The United Methodist Publishing House, 1989.

Heavilin, Marilyn Willett. "Is That You Lord?" *Pray!*, no. 13 (1999).

Miller, J. Lane and Madeleine S. *Harper's Bible Dictionary*. New York, Evanston, and London: Harper & Row, 1961.

Poinsett, Brenda. "Jesus' Inferred Prayers." *Pray!*, no. 14 (1999).

Poinsett, Brenda. "Why Did Jesus Pray?" *Pray!*, no. 14 (1999.

Spirit Filled Life Bible, Nashville, TN: Thomas Nelson, 1991.

Wallis, Arthur. *God's Chosen Fast, A Spiritual and Practical Guide to Fasting.* Fort Washington, PA: Christian Literature Crusade, 1975.

Webster's New Collegiate Dictionary. Springfield, MA: G. & C. Merriam, 1959.

Webster's New World Dictionary of the American Language, Second College Edition, New York, NY: Simon and Schuster, 1984.

Lord, Teach Us to Pray Seminar

We read in the gospels of Jesus teaching the disciples many things. We only read of one instance where the disciples asked Jesus to teach them about something. In Luke 11:1 when Jesus finished praying in a certain place, one of his disciples requested, "Lord, teach us to pray, as John taught his disciples." In observing the prayer life of Jesus, the disciples sensed that they had a lot more to learn about prayer and that Jesus' prayer life was the key to the powerful ministry that he had. What about you?

- Do you have the sense that your prayer life needs improvement?

- Do you need to learn how to pray more effectively?

- Do you sense that improving your prayer life would improve your ministry for Jesus?

- Is your personal prayer life a duty, a discipline, or a delight?

- Does your personal prayer life reflect an intimate relationship with the Lord that is growing and maturing?

- Do you yearn to have a closer walk with the Lord through prayer?

- Do you use the tools for personal prayer that can make your prayer life exciting and vibrant?
- Do you experience obstacles or hindrances to intimacy with God through prayer?

Here are some evaluations from other pastors and participants who attended a Lord, Teach Us to Pray seminar in their local church.

- Pastor: A step of growth in our prayer life. I've seen it already as people pray in groups and meetings.
- Pastor: The highlight for me was watching the interaction and enthusiasm of the participants in the prayer exercises and in worship.
- Participant: I felt the leaders exemplified a genuine love for prayer, and communicated the fact that everyone can learn to pray.
- Participant: The highlight for the church was evident from the looks of pure joy and huge smiles on the faces of every person as they received their anointing to be "people of prayer."
- Participant: I learned that I hadn't been allowing God his turn. The one thing I will do differently is listen to God in the stillness of each day.

Aldersgate Renewal Ministries
121 East Avenue, Goodlettsville, TN 37072
Phone: 615-851-9192   Fax: 615-851-9372
E-mail: Info@AldersgateRenewal.org
Web Page: www.AldersgateRenewal.org